MW01205220

All I Wanted Was A Home

Raised in an Orphanage

Kym

I had your new found interest in reading in mind when I wrote this book — I hope I am correct.

Clark
6/09
Austin

Clark Watts

authorHOUSE®

AuthorHouse™
1663 Liberty Drive
Bloomington, IN 47403
www.authorhouse.com
Phone: 1-800-839-8640

First published by AuthorHouse 4/23/2009

ISBN: 978-1-4389-6947-3 (sc)
ISBN: 978-1-4389-6948-0 (hc)

Printed in the United States of America
Bloomington, Indiana

This book is printed on acid-free paper.

To my sister Eva

Who wanted me to write this book,

who didn't get to see this book,

who would have, I hope, enjoyed this book.

Contents

PREFACE

I was raised in Buckner Orphans Home near Dallas, Texas. This is my story. It is told through a series of tales, each of which reveals something about the operation of the institution and its impact on me. I have recreated these adventures for several reasons.

Principally, I make this record for my family, for two reasons. First, there existed no concentrated source of information about my family prior to this rendition. Thus, it serves as a starting point for anyone interested in the story of the family. The second and more important reason I have written this account is to fulfill a promise I made to my younger sister, Eva, who asked me repeatedly to write this book, and to whom I repeatedly promised I would. Unfortunately, she did not live to see it.

She was an award-winning schoolteacher of preadolescent children, a responsibility that occupied most of her adult life, taking her from Dallas through Native American reservations in New Mexico to the outback of Australia and back. She never married. As a teacher myself, I spent hours discussing the art and science of teaching with her, and became aware of her basic philosophy about teaching and learning. Neither could be accomplished if the teacher was not respected, and the teacher would not be respected if he did not keep his word. I have done so.

This writing was also influenced by another dynamic. In telling some of these stories to others over the years, it has become clear to me that few knew of the way of life about which I write. Furthermore, inquiry has led me to discover that there has been revived, dormant for more than a quarter of a century, a discussion of the value of orphanages in our society. From one viewpoint, they are portrayed as mere warehouses of children in which untold horrors have been inflicted upon the inmates. Others, including former inhabitants, however, suggest they may be a suitable option for some children currently in our foster care system, which has its problems. Perhaps my experience will be a useful contribution to that discussion.

The material in the book is mine, gleaned entirely from my memory of events over fifty years ago. Any factual errors are mine, but I hope the reader will be tolerant of me and my memory if he or she finds deviations from his or her own recollections; and I expect there will be some. To pre-empt debate of any differences between my recollections and those of others, I have concluded that a writer, sincere in his subject, should be presumed to have recounted accurately the essential facts existing only in memory of events over fifty years old, recognizing that this doctrine has not been established by scientific scrutiny or philosophical analysis. Though I subscribe to that dictum, I have largely avoided the use of dialogue or personal names in my stories in order not to associate others with facts that may be in question. However, I have not tried to disguise the identity of any participant.

ACKNOWLEDGMENTS

The creation of this book was delayed too long; the blame for this is mine alone. While over the years others have followed Eva in encouraging me to write the book, responsibility for igniting the commencing spark lay with Dr. Sal Fiscina and his wife Jo-Ann who, during a vacation I spent at their home on the eastern shore of the Chesapeake Bay, convinced me of the importance of family history to progeny. The effort then became irreversible due to the energetic and infectious encouragement of Dr. Melissa Neiman, whose entreaties that I must do this simply could not be ignored.

My wife Patricia, provided that intangible personal support without which, to put it bluntly, I would have failed. Gerald Livingston, a friend of over forty years, contributed valuable critique as the stories evolved, as did Dr. William Wellborn and Dr. Patricia Aronin. Former inhabitants of the orphanage have responded with candor to my queries for which I am pleased, including Gordon John Ratcliff, Sammy Sims, Nettie Jo Woods McLeod, Wanda Joyce McKinney Baker, and Jerre Graves Simmons. Dr. Tom McConnell is due special recognition; he was constantly whispering in my ear about adjectives. And the insightful and sensitive editing of Erin Brown is the reason I am pleased to share this product with my family, critics unmatched.

Finally, although this is not intended to be a scholarly treatise, I have listed as references works to which I have looked for specific information, of which the reader might want to know the source.

INTRODUCTION

Buckner Orphans Home was founded by Robert Cooke Buckner (1833-1919) in Dallas County, Texas, in 1879. He, with the support of a group of Baptist ministers that preceded the Southern Baptist Convention, purchased the first parcel of land on which the orphanage came to reside, in 1880. Notable in the growth of the orphanage along with the reputation of Dr. Buckner was the addition of nearly one hundred children to the rolls of the institution after the Galveston hurricane in 1900 (Bullock,1993).

Buckner was a large institution in 1947 when I arrived. It held about 750 children, with 600 of school age in grades one to twelve. While the main campus consisted of approximately fifty acres, Buckner had roughly 3,000 acres of land for pasture, cultivation, and what is known today as green space. Besides the activities on the main campus, there was a dairy that provided the milk required by the children, and a farm that managed the cultivated lands and the non-dairy cattle. The farm operations were conducted from a compound consisting of two houses for the employees, barns for various purposes, and corrals for working the cattle. It lay just north of the main campus across Highway 80, an extension east of Samuels Boulevard from Dallas. The dairy was situated principally north of Highway 80 about one mile west of the main campus. It was dominated by the large milking barn, which could hold up to one hundred cows awaiting their turns. Also on the property were two silos attached to the barn, a couple of houses for the employees, and an artificial pond of about an acre, which had no practical purpose; it was just there. On both sites were buildings in which the moveable equipment including tractors and trucks were stored.

The main campus, where the children lived, was a self-contained community. The 150 preschool children were housed and cared for—separate from the older children—in Sunbeam Home, a two-story building on the south edge of the main campus with its own fenced space, near the hospital. Their attendants were adults permanently and exclusively assigned to their care, who were assisted by some of the older girls who lived in the orphanage.

The school-age children were housed in buildings on the main campus separated by gender, and within the buildings on floors by age. The boys were in buildings on the north side of the campus and the girls on the south. Initially, there were two, two-story and two, three-story buildings on each side. By the time I reached high school, a third two-story building was added to each side. With few exceptions, each floor of a building contained about thirty children overseen by a female adult who lived on the floor. From time to time some of the floors of the older children were managed by married couples. All the children ate at the same time in the community dining room, Manna Hall. Thus, it was necessary the children arrive and be seated on time and with order. The younger ones were marched from their buildings single file to the dining room at each meal; the older children followed in less formal, but nevertheless orderly groups.

Provisions for all the needs of the children, whether in the dining room served by a huge kitchen or in the separate living areas, were supplied from the commissary. Its bakery is remembered fondly by all, especially for its breads and pastries. The schools, the church, the gymnasium and football field, and a hospital were on the main campus. The dairy and the farm operations supplied some of the needs of the children. But most of the needs of the children were provided through generous donations from the Baptist community. This was especially important at Christmas when each child received his own present, with his name on it, containing articles of need along with those of joy.

The rather large child to adult ratio, often thirty or more children per adult, might suggest the adults could have difficulty controlling the children without instituting harsh measures of "crowd" control, given the background of broken homes most of the children brought with them to the Home, the name most used for the institution. This was not the case. I witnessed no major events of group unrest, with a rather mild exception seen when boys were told to wait tables in the dining hall (developed in the tale, "Girls' Work"), nor do I recall the use of oppressive measures to control groups of children. I have no memory of discussing this issue while in the Home or afterwards, or even giving it much thought at the time. But as I look back I attribute this state of affairs to an attitude I brought with me to the Home. I saw a comfortable place, in many ways more so than any I had previously experienced. I welcomed it, especially its offer of security and stability along with permanency. I did not want to do anything that might jeopardize my situation. I believe this principle was widely felt by most of the children. The peace of the place was policed by the children themselves, with the older children showing their contentment to the younger through their behavior. As a result very few children were turned out, usually to the custody of rather reluctant relatives, because of behavioral problems.

FAMILY MATTERS

My brother Clyde and I entered Buckner Orphans Home in late summer of 1947; my sisters Anne, Orene, and Eva came later, but in time for the start of the school year. Clyde left the Home early and enlisted in the U.S. Marine Corps; the rest of us stayed and graduated from high school. However, for reasons developed in this account, each of us led lives in the orphanage largely independent of each other. Our younger sister, Paula, did not accompany us into the Home. Mother decided to have her raised by an aunt, Mother's oldest sister, and her husband; they had not been able to have children. In reaching the Home, the path we took was distinctive in its course, but not remarkable. Most of the children in the Home were not orphans; they had at least one parent and other relatives. But they, as we, came from broken homes. The major reason we came to the home was poverty, with no other way out. The stories of others were truly heartbreaking, with violence, even murder, the cause of the family breakdown. Quite important to the function of the orphanage was that no child was admitted to the Home because of behavioral or delinquency difficulties. It was not a warehouse for problem children.

****

First Memories

The exact dates of the following events are unknown to me, and I have no way of accessing them. Mother died in 1994, and left no diary or helpful papers. My memory is my only guide, and it revealed that the earliest significant family effort was a move, in late 1942 or early 1943, from Texas to live in California. The family consisted of my father and mother, my siblings Orene, Anne, and Clyde, and me. Father's name was Clyde; my brother was the Third. The move was an attempt on my father's part to find work, so he told me after we arrived in California. I do not recall the car my father drove, but the trip was uneventful

On the trip I accidentally dropped a WWII German helmet out the window of the car; Father would not stop to pick it up. I do not recall how I came to possess it, but he must have told me to be careful, and I wasn't. It had a hole in it, which I came to believe was from a bullet. My uncle James had fought in Europe, and may have been the source. I recall little else of the trip to California except for a fascination with miles and miles of orange groves, extending to the horizon. Father, on a few occasions, stopped and we gathered some of the fruit. How or why he knew it was proper to do this was a mystery to me, but we casually spread a blanket by the side of the road and enjoyed some of the fruit before continuing on our way.

We lived in Fresno, California, on a wide street with date palm trees in the center of an island of parkland separating the two lanes of the street. Our house had a large fig tree in the back. Its growth was such that it resembled a cave from underneath, where I spent a good part of my time. The only problems were the wasps the fruit attracted; we left each other alone. I recall nothing of substance about our family life, or my school experience, except for Rachel. A redhead, she was the largest kid in my first grade class. For some reason, there were several boys who did not like me, and who projected, by word and by body language, an interest in causing me harm on the way home from school. Rachel took it upon herself to provide protection; she lived near my house and walked home with me every day.

My father, according to my mother, did not get to high school. The only job I recall he had was delivering milk to stores in towns around Fresno. Occasionally, I went with him on his routes. He would sit me in his lap and let me steer the truck, even in the hills. In pictures I saw later, he appeared about six feet tall, slim, dark headed, and very handsome. I remember him as being without humor, but patient, and rather quiet. One day he directed me to walk with him down the street. He was carrying a small satchel that he often took on his milk route when he was going to be away overnight. When we reached the corner, he told me that he was going to have to leave us. Simply put, he was unable to provide for us. By then Eva had been born, as had Josephine who died in infancy of pneumonia, and Mother was pregnant with Paula. He told me that as the oldest I would have to help Mother look after us. He turned and walked away. I watched him for a few minutes, until he disappeared around the next block. I now feel nothing. I don't recall feeling anything at the time; I must have been numb. I went home and told Mother what had happened. She cried briefly, softly, and said everything would be all right.

Sometime later, we took a bus back to Ft. Worth, Texas, where relatives lived. I believe the trip was taken in the summer of 1945, as Paula was born in Ft. Worth in November of that year, and I was able to enter school without interruption. Although Mother worked hard to keep us together, we spent most of our time separated, living with various relatives. I spent some time in two orphanages in Ft. Worth. I was alone at All Church Home; Clyde may have been with me at Lena Pope Home. Eventually, the decision was made to place us in Buckner.

****

Arrival

I do not recall the date we arrived at Buckner, but it was in early August in 1947, during the middle of the week; I was nine years old. We approached the Home, as we learned to call it, by car from the south on Buckner Boulevard. About a mile from the main entrance into the campus, we topped a small hill, giving us our first view. Clyde and I were in the backseat, Mother was in the passenger seat, and our aunt was driving. I do not have any emotional memories of those moments. Perhaps I was not especially disturbed, because of the time I spent in the two orphanages in Ft. Worth during the two years after our return to Texas from California. Clyde, twenty months younger than I, was asleep.

My first impression was that the place resembled pictures of California prisons I had seen in magazines. There were a number of red brick buildings. Trees abounded— some as tall as the tallest buildings— but fewer, given the size of the place, than I had seen in the Ft. Worth institutions. A tall water tower was visible beyond the buildings to the east. The nearest buildings were perhaps one hundred yards away from the edge of the property, marked by a chain-linked fence about four feet high, near the highway. I remarked silently to myself that I did not see any guard towers. Also, I did not see people, at first. I subsequently learned that we had approached, initially, the girls' side of the campus, and they did not play in the fields in the summer.

As I made these observations, we passed the main entrance to the campus. The gate was obscured from the road by tall green bushes, and at our car speed, we passed before I had a chance to truly observe the gate. I did notice a small one-story brick building adjacent to the gate. Immediately beyond the gate I saw several boys in the fields between the buildings and the fence. Approaching the north extent of the campus, where Buckner Boulevard intersected Samuels Boulevard, I saw two boys draped over the fence; one waved, but I just looked. Only then did I perceive a disquieting inner discomfort. I would be meeting boys like those soon enough; how would I be received? And the place was bigger than that which I had experienced before. I told myself this place was going to be different; I did not dwell on how different. But I sensed that the rather chaotic and somewhat nomadic life I had lived the past two years was over.

We turned right on Samuels, and after about a quarter mile, turned left into a driveway at the end of which stood a two-story brick building. We had arrived; this was the Receiving Home. Clyde and I would live here for the next two weeks, in quarantine, to be watched for the appearance of any disease that could spread to others when we moved to the main campus. Mother had been quiet during most of the trip. Occasionally I heard whispering between her and our aunt, but I could not ascertain what they said; the road noise accompanied by the noise of the wind through the open car windows was prohibitive. But as we progressed up the driveway, I could hear my mother quietly crying. Our aunt said something about turning around and coming back another day; Mother simply shook her head. From her reaction I deduced I was correct—this was going to be different, was going to be permanent.

We stopped just short of the building, where a concrete walk greeted us and on which we made our way towards the front entrance to the building, escorted by a lovely row of yellow and red flowers bordering the walk. Before we advanced more than halfway to the receiving porch, two people—a somewhat overweight lady and a slim man the same height as the woman, and both to me of indeterminate age—exited the front door and approached us. Our aunt immediately assumed control of the situation, making introductions; Mother assumed the position of a passive bystander. Initially, Clyde and I stood quietly on the sidewalk, while the adults talked; it seemed they were continuing a conversation that had begun at an earlier time. Clyde soon became restless and needed to go to the bathroom. I was momentarily curious as to the discussion among the adults, but when it became obvious they were not concerned about our immediate status, I took him by the hand and led him to a bench that sat in front of a thick green bush in the yard. He relieved himself behind the bush. Viewed years later, it seems that he provided a marker with this first act by which his attitude toward the orphanage could have been predicted.

When they took us into the building, they showed us a room with four beds. At the time we were the only ones housed in the Receiving Home, but one other boy came during our second week. Mother hugged each of us, but could say nothing. Our aunt told us that if we needed anything the people there knew how to reach her and my mother. My aunt gave to the man a paper sack which contained some clothes of ours, then she and mother left. Clyde immediately went to his bed and lay down. I spent a few minutes looking around to get my bearings.

Our aunt brought Mother the next weekend for a brief visit. We were told that Mother might be able to get a job at the Home and then would be with us everyday. While at the Receiving Home, I remember spending a great deal of time in the front yard looking across Samuels Boulevard at the Home, wondering about it. I recall nothing else; such is the nature of most colorless beginnings.

****

Together

After two weeks in quarantine at the Receiving Home (Samuel H. Payne Hall), a building just north of the main campus across Samuel Boulevard, Clyde and I were settled into our permanent quarters on the main campus: Pires dormitory (or dorm), the building for the youngest school-age boys. Once my status in school was settled, I was moved forward to the building appropriate for my age and class, Freeland dorm. Anne, after her stay at the Receiving Home, was housed in Hunt dorm with other girls her age. Mother was able to get a job at the Home helping to take care of the 150 preschool children, including Eva and Orene in Sunbeam Home. She had a room in Curtis Home, a building next to Sunbeam. When she was off duty she could have all of us visit in her quarters, and walk with her anywhere she wanted to go on campus. We spent a great deal of this time sitting under trees, listening to Mother read the Bible and talk about Jesus. She professed to no specific religious denomination, eventually associating herself with several branches of Protestantism.

Undoubtedly, this time with her allowed us to settle in without much angst. However, it was during this time that I experienced the only persistent negative reaction from my peers at the Home during the eight years of my stay. Because we were with Mother, we were able to move about the campus and to visit freely with each other. The campus was large, over fifty acres, and the boys and girls, especially at our ages, had little opportunity to visit and intermingle except on special occasions. Mother's presence on campus provided those occasions; unfortunately, but perhaps understandably, some less fortunate were resentful.

Her close presence was most auspicious when it came time for me to start school in September. I was nine years old, and the authorities assigned me to the fourth grade. I had attended the fourth grade in Ft. Worth, so I asked Mother why I had to repeat the grade. She became most upset and went immediately to the school for discussions, the substance of which I am unaware. I do know, she told me later, that in California I was a good student and had been promoted from first to third grade, skipping the second. So, when we moved back to Texas, I attended the third grade, and the fourth before entering Buckner. The result of her conference was that I was assigned to the fifth grade, with the admonition that I had to be a good student and study hard. During my time at the Home, I was always the youngest student in my class, one of the smallest boy until my sophomore year in high school, and academically at the top of the class.

Mother maintained her job there for two years, then left to take a position as a secretary in Dallas. She, throughout the next two to three years, visited us almost weekly. Later as we grew older, her visits were less often; she had her own life to live and we had adjusted well to life in the Home. She never revealed to me that she had ever heard form our father.

****

Sunday

At the orphanage, Sunday mornings were devoted to the Southern Baptist tradition of worship. It began with Sunday school, where the kids were taught the basic principles of Baptist doctrine in classes conducted similarly to those in the secular school. All children participated; the older boys and girls either attended classes for their age groups, or served as teaching assistants in classes for younger children. Church services in the Chapel followed; evening worship services were held after dinner. In my senior year I was selected to perform tasks for the church administrative offices, which exempted me from Sunday school and, frequently, church services. The majority of my work consisted of clerical matters concerning the church. In addition, on occasion, I escorted visitors who wished to see various aspects of life at the Home. Consequently, each Sunday I appeared in a white shirt and tie at the church administrative offices on the second floor of the annex, above the Manna Hall and behind the church, to fulfill my responsibilities.

I liked Sunday. We had few chores, beyond the care of our personal living spaces. Everyone prepared for the biblical day of rest. After Sunday school and church services in the morning, the afternoon was reserved for visitations by family and friends of the children, if there were any. This day was also a day when the older children, at least those in high school, had an opportunity to practice their evolving social skills. The boys could visit with their girlfriends in the parlor of the girls' buildings, with an adult, usually a matron of the building, sitting in a rather conspicuous spot in the parlor.

The church services held in the evening after dinner were attended by all but the youngest of the school-age children. As previously noted, the older boys were permitted to escort their girlfriends home to their buildings, with adults strategically placed between church and those buildings to monitor the pace of the walk in the dark. Later the boys— at least some of them, and it seemed the same ones every week—would regale us with their successes in stealing kisses from under the watchful eyes of the roving chaperones. The stories were simple enough and only half believed, but the relater was nevertheless congratulated, especially if it was his first time. The state of innocence was such that these boys, when pressed for more details, invariably regressed to embarrassed and self-conscious mutism. On Sundays, the world seemed different; and on one particular Sunday, it *was* different.

On that winter day, when I arrived, the expected guests had not yet appeared, so I was asked to go over the books reflecting the previous Sunday's data of attendance, collections, visitations, baptisms, and related annotations. I was working, standing at a tall counter with my back to the door, when it opened. Strangely, I was stricken with a sudden chill that ran from my upper chest to somewhere deep within my lower abdomen. I remain convinced it was not due to the brief puff of cold air admitted through the door; the door had been opened previously without notice as others came and went. The chill yielded to a sense of anxiety I had before never experienced. The data on the sheets before me became incomprehensible. My brain clearly was failing to understand what had possessed me. Out of the corner of my eye, to my right, I saw a man approach the counter, moving slowly with a shuffling gait. He did not turn toward me, but instead asked the girl directly in front of him behind the counter if she knew how he could speak with Clark Watts. Her eyes, widened by the spectacle before her, turned to me; otherwise she did not move; nor did she say a word. Stiffly, almost mechanically, I turned toward him and introduced myself.

He obviously was experiencing hard times. His hair, dark brown with liberal quantities of gray, was long and poorly combed. He had a beard that also contained much gray, was several days old, and not trimmed. He wore a faded, dark blue suit without a tie and a long, brown well-worn but clean overcoat. When I spoke his body tensed slightly and he withdrew from me a half step. I felt he was unsure how to handle the situation. It seemed as if he did not expect to benefit from his request so quickly; he did not have time to prepare himself. I recovered even as he was becoming unsettled. I directed him to follow me into a room just off the foyer. I did not know what this was about and I wanted privacy, as much for myself as for him.

He told me he was James Watts, my father's older brother, and that he had come to see how we were doing. He had been informed of our location by my mother. Over the next few minutes, we became more comfortable with each other, with small talk about the Home and how we were doing. I did not ask about our father—I did not care to know—but he told me he had seen him in El Paso a few years past on a construction job. I did not probe. He volunteered my father's health was good, and that Father did not mention us when they met. He was not forthcoming, and I did not ask, as to specifically why he was here. He did ask to see the others. I made a few telephone calls, and arranged for us to see my siblings in their buildings. This would not happen until the afternoon, after church services and lunch, so I escorted him to the Maris Welcome Center across campus where he could wait. He had available to him coffee, soft drinks, and comfortable chairs until I re-joined him for the visits.

And so I spent that Sunday afternoon. We walked from building to building, girls' side and boys', and visited with each: Clyde, Anne, Orene, Eva. Without exception, the meetings were awkward. My siblings knew the meetings were important because I was there. However, there was nothing to bind us, no common frame of reference from which relaxed meaningful discourse could evolve. Clearly, each kid was relieved when I declared it was time for us to leave. For myself, I felt it necessary the visitations occur. I did not know why, which was probably why I carried with me such a small emotional burden as we made our rounds. As we encountered people I knew on the campus, who invariably with facial expressions and other body language posed the expected questions, I said nothing but simply nodded as we passed. Later, when questioned, I pled personal privacy. I did not want to explain, as I was not sure where such discussions would go, but I knew I was unprepared to go there.

I never saw him or heard from him again.

ZERO UNEMPLOYMENT

Every school-age child at Buckner had work to do. Each took care of his or her personal space, including bed and closet. And all participated in keeping the building in which they lived clean. This included performing work in the gardens immediately surrounding the buildings. But Buckner, as an institution, was more than buildings and living space. It was a self-contained community, with a large kitchen, laundry, bakery, commissary, dairy, and farming operation to support the needs of the inhabitants of the buildings. Although adults were hired to oversee the conduct of these activities, the children were essential to the success of the operations. From the fifth grade, or from ages ten to twelve depending on the child's size, he or she was assigned work in one of these areas. I do not recall how the initial assignments were made—they were usually decided after consultation with the appropriate housemother and work manager, but without consulting the child—but repeat assignments often took the child's desires into consideration, especially as the child grew older. As a result many children eventually left the Home with the skills necessary to work in a trade represented by one of the required work assignments.

****

Field Gang

There were no unemployment lines for the children in the Home. The youngest boys, in Pires dorm, took care of their personal belongings and their living spaces. This included scrubbing the concrete floors with soap and water on Saturday, with the boys often working on their knees. The older boys, in addition to taking care of their personal space, had jobs in the Buckner community. My first such job was in the Field Gang. I was ten years old, and the youngest and smallest kid in the gang. But size was not that important with this job, which consisted of keeping the campus clean and neat. The younger children, with the prodding of the matrons who lived with them and oversaw their lives, took care of the gardens immediately around their buildings; the work was often punishment for some transgression. The buildings in which the older boys lived didn't have gardens, unless the adults who lived there took care of them. The Field Gang took care of everything else, the common grounds. In the summer we mowed the grass and cut the weeds. All year round, except when there was snow on the ground, we swept the streets clean, every Saturday. An older boy, the boss, oversaw us.

The grass mower was hand pushed, without an engine. The cutting blades were mounted between the wheels, which supplied the mechanical power when the mower was pushed. The key to using this machine was adjusting the blades so that all mowers cut the grass at a certain length. It would not be appropriate for the grass to be mowed with ten mowers, each cutting the grass at a different length. Adjusting the blades was the most important job of the boss. The lawn was mowed as we moved in an open V configuration, similar to that of migrating geese. This technique was fast and efficient; we mowed several acres every week in the middle of summer. Others, at the same time, trimmed the edges of walks and pulled weeds.

We swept the streets in a similar configuration. In the middle of the street was the point man. Welding the broom as he walked at a leisurely pace, he swept the portion of the street confronting him with strokes of the broom moving side to side. On either side of him was another boy sweeping his portion of the street, including the debris previously swept into his path by the point man. The boy to the right of the point man swept to his right and the boy to the left to his left. Staggered in that way were three or four boys on each side. Eventually the street debris reached the curb. Trailing the sweepers, on each side of the street, was a team of two or three boys with a wheelbarrow. With brooms and a shovel, they picked the debris up and placed it into the wheelbarrow, which was emptied at select points along the route, to be picked up later with the trash from the various buildings. There were about 1.5 miles of streets to be swept each week.

Field gang work was hot and sweaty in the summer and often most uncomfortable in the wind and cold of winter. But we did not want visitors to see unkempt lawns and dirty streets on Sunday. I recall with pride hearing compliments from the pulpit on how the campus looked. Besides a source of pride and a mark of accomplishment, the work was sometimes fun. We usually were able to take our time and enjoy the company of the group. Give young boys brooms and shovels in the presence of dirt, and high jinks are born. In the usual operation the boy was bent over, a position that invited creative and playful use of the broom handle. We gossiped, told entertaining stories and jokes, and visited with kids on other parts of the campus, meaning the girls. From time to time, they would bring us cool water and something to eat. On such occasions, we remained vigilant in case one of the boys became too friendly with a girl; this behavior became fodder for later comments, the contents unique to boys at that age. But perhaps the best part of the experience came much later, when we looked back and noted the role this work had in teaching us the value of having a job—even a job requiring few skills but requiring teamwork—and doing it well.

****

Girls' Work

Even the girls had jobs. I do not recall, if I ever knew, what the youngest girls did with their floors, but I knew the older girls, like the boys, had chores outside their buildings. Most of them worked in the laundry, the kitchen, or the dining hall. I had little exposure to the laundry, but I recall seeing the girls operating presses, ironing shirts, and managing the washing machines in a building without air conditioning, only overhead fans and open windows.

I spent a great deal of time observing the work of the girls in the kitchen and the dining room, because we ate three meals a day there. Manna Hall was huge, permitting almost 600 children to be seated each meal. The tables resembled large picnic tables, with a plank attached to each side on which the diners sat. The diners at each table were served by one older girl, who was seated in a separate chair at the head of the table. After a hymn was sung by all, accompanied on the piano by a student (usually a girl as there were only a few boys who studied piano in school) and a prayer, the service began. The girl assigned to each table would go to the kitchen, which was centrally located on the east side of the dining space, and pick up the food to bring to the table. The table had been set after the previous meal with, at each place, a plate, a cup that was white and opaque, and spoon, fork, and knife.

The food in individual bowls was passed around the table for each diner to help himself; the waitress helped the smaller ones and controlled the aggressive ones. This worked well at the tables where the younger girls dined, less well where the older boys dined, and in between, in between. The waitress, depending upon the meal, might return to the kitchen once or twice for additional food. The food was plentiful, but there were no obese children in the orphanage.

As one might expect, at times there were moments of tension at the tables where the older boys ate, depending on the character, the personality, and the physical appearance of the waitress, and the energy level with which she carried out her job. The behavior of the boys ranged from gentle teasing or overt flirting to harassment, or worse. The boys were able to so torment a girl they did not want at their table, regardless the reason, that she would leave in humiliation with a not so enthusiastic replacement to follow. One simple act of harassment was to turn all the cups upside down on a morning when hot chocolate was served. One half of the cups would be empty, but one half would be filled with chocolate.* The decision by the waitress when it came time to clean the table was how to pick up a cup which may or may not contain chocolate, and how to control the chocolate if contained within the cup. And there were as many as ten cups awaiting her decision. A more malicious act was for one of the boys to surreptitiously cause a plate or bowl, filled with food, to fall to the floor and then to loudly proclaim the waitress the perpetrator. The first accusation was immediately followed by several more at such a volume, with finger pointing, the girl would leave in tears.

But then came a time of reckoning; one summer the adults determined it was time to teach the boys lessons of civility, if not humility. Without preliminary consultation it was decided boys, largely from Rupert dorm, would service the boys' tables; they were to serve the meals and clean afterwards. The waiters were selected and the experiment began. The initial phase of the work shift, the procurement of the food, went without many problems. There was some silly talk between the boys and girls when they mingled to obtain the food: "where is your dress?" or "cute outfit" to boys wearing overalls, "watch it muscles" or "may I help you darling?" to the thin girl struggling with her tray of food. It was a totally expected and, some thought promising, beginning.

Soon, however, it became apparent this attempt at social engineering was misguided. After the first week the inventory of table dishes was cut significantly due to breakage. The boys tested the theory that a dish could be tossed from table to table like a Frisbee (not yet invented); the toss was easy, the catch was not. The glass plates were replaced with those made of tin. Each had the potential of becoming a discus loaded with food. Some did, with no air space exempted in the dining hall. The tin plates were rapidly replaced with paper plates, which were folded and converted into missiles loaded with food and launched from one table to another by opposing groups of boys committed to the common goal of defeating this progressive social experiment.

The floor was turned into a combined skating rink and slalom run from the soapy dishwater spilled at every table, and along the route from the kitchen where the bucket of water for dishwashing was retrieved and the table where the washing took place. Competitions were held between waiters as to who could slide the farthest, or who could cause another to slide the farthest, after it was determined by way of a scrum resembling a tag-team wrestling match, who would be slid.

This state of affairs developed and matured over a period of about two weeks, starting slowly with the first innocently spilt bucket of water, and the first airborne dish. The initial reactions were relatively mooted—suppressed laughter from the girls and a steady stare from the manager of the kitchen/dining hall complex. The state of anarchy rapidly evolved into stark pandemonium by the end of the first week, with the stare now accompanied by a crossing of the arms on the chest, and matured into indescribable chaos by the beginning of the second; the stare was now accompanied by a blood curdling vocal response, which some called a squeal of anguish and others a death gasp, with the loss of each plate.

By this time disorder began spreading into the area of the dining hall where the girls ate and worked. First came the paper plate missiles; then the trails of water as the boys took circuitous routes from the kitchen with their water buckets to avoid the challenge of others with grievances. While none of the girls were engaged physically, their increasingly heightened state of alertness diminished their efficiency. Although adults were assigned to patrol the hall during cleanup, they could not see behind their backs. Nor could they maintain the dignity of authority when they unexpectedly encountered and succumbed to the skating rink/slalom runs. Nightly "discussions" held in the dorm with the boys by the authorities ended with the consensus, of the boys, that boys were not put on earth to do the tasks of waiting on others; they were to be waited upon. Furthermore, the results of this experiment established to be true, the consensus continued, the proposition that boys were not emotionally or psychologically constituted, nor physically coordinated, to work with soap, water, and dishes.

The experiment ended as abruptly as it began. After-action analysis revealed nothing was changed, no life lessons were learned. But confirmed beyond the startling finding that boys and soap, water, and dishes do not mix well, was that the chore of serving meals, including the restoration of order and cleanliness in the aftermath, was not within the circumscription, or genetic footprint, of the young male.

---

* Rather easy to accomplish. First, the mouth of the cup, ¾ full of chocolate, is covered with paper, preferably waxed. The cup is held in the right hand (the left if one is left-handed) and the left hand is placed flat on top of the paper. With both hands the cup is turned rapidly upside down. Then the edge of the left hand, now on the bottom of the construct, is placed flush against the edge of the table. The cup is slid, along with the paper, onto the table from the left hand with the right hand and a little help from a collaborator. The paper is removed from underneath the cup. Voila! Un problème magnifique.

****

Turkeys

The children in the orphanage did not lack for material goods, especially as certain days important to Southern Baptists approached. This was particularly noted during the two weeks or so leading to Thanksgiving. From throughout northeast and eastern Texas, trucks arrived almost daily bringing live turkeys donated so the children would have turkey at dinner on Thanksgiving Day. On the weekend before the day, the orphans were in control of dozens of turkeys. Since there was no permanent place to hold them and since they would ultimately be brought to the kitchen to be prepared, they were placed in a temporary shelter constructed of wire mesh in a small vacant area south of the commissary, immediately across the street from the kitchen. Eventually, all became aware of the turkeys; their presence was a delight to the younger children, who were brought by their matrons to see them. The question floating just under the surface of this awareness was who was going to kill them.

The kitchen was the busiest daily operation on the campus. Almost 600 children, along with twenty-five to thirty adults, were fed three meals per day every day of the year. And they were fed at the same time, in Manna Hall. As with all operations, children of a certain age performed the majority of the work under the supervision of adults. The kitchen was the responsibility of the girls, and was supplied from the commissary, which was immediately across the street, along with the bakery, both manned by boys. The manager of the kitchen and the Manna Hall was a notable lady of unknown origin. She was tall, slim, of indeterminate age, with long black hair usually wrapped around her head but occasionally allowed to hang down her back where it extended below the waist; she was frightening to all she encountered, especially the younger girls meeting her for the first time. A simple glance from her was reported to cause some of them to swoon. The boys, who never had to deal with her up close, but who were filled with the rumors of her that abounded—consistent with their more salacious characterizations of her—would sing the popular song honoring a birthday under her window on Halloween night as part of their search for tricks or treats.

She had a difficult and important responsibility, which she carried out without fanfare and without failure. The daily menus were set, and were repeated weekly. Lunch on Sunday consisted of roast beef cut into cubes of roughly one inch, with mashed potatoes and gravy. Dinner on Thursday invariably brought gravy and slices of white bread along with lemon pie. Milk and water were served with each meal. The girls worked at large stoves and ovens, taking hours to prepare a meal, serve it, and clean up afterwards. I had no direct experience with these tasks, but I observed them up close when I worked at the commissary and delivered the supplies. I noted almost from the first day on the job at the commissary that the girls did not have the time or the desire to engage in idle chat. This was especially true at 4:30 a.m. on Sunday morning when they arrived in the kitchen to peel potatoes for lunch. Because of the affect of heat and humidity on their personal appearances, it was clear they desired we made our presence as short as possible.

The commissary contained among other features large walk-in refrigerators and freezers where the food was kept; it also had a large ice-making facility yielding blocks of ice weighing one hundred pounds. Eventually, the commissary contained a pasteurizing plant for the milk produced at the dairy. It was quite an undertaking to select the supplies and to get them to the kitchen each day at the proper time. The uniformity and predictability of the daily menu made the chore easier, but the sheer volume compounded the task. The arrival of days for special meals was anticipated by all those who consumed, not by those who produced. Of course those who did both were conflicted. One of those times of conflict was when the turkeys were prepared for Thanksgiving dinner.

First, they had to be killed. I was the appointed executioner one season. I worked in the commissary, and was old enough but not too old. The adults, it seems, made some effort at times like this to fit the individual to the job. The boy in charge had to be able to control those working with him, but not of an age where his peers felt he was performing an activity beneath his stage of maturity. The process was simple, but filled with action. Several smaller boys had to enter the shelter with me, and catch the birds, one at a time. Some of the birds were quite large and it required two, sometimes three boys, to capture one of them and bring it to me. The boys lay on the bird to keep it still. Its neck was stretched across a wooden slab by traction applied to its head. With one stroke I severed the neck with a hand axe. Instantly the bird was released. Contrary to the myth, the bird did not get up and run without its head. Instead its entire body engaged in a series of irregular spasms, spewing blood from the neck as it flopped around on the ground. This allowed the body to be drained of blood, a result desired by the cooks. We did not have enough trees to carry out the traditional form of execution where the bird was tied upside down to a branch and its throat slit, allowing the blood to drain away. After the bird became still it was placed in a large washtub filled with hot water almost at the boiling point. This soaking made it easier to remove the feathers. From this point on the bird was the responsibility of the cooks.

Because I worked at the commissary, I was able to obtain the most important of the required equipment for myself and crew, old clothes that would never be used again. Everyone became covered with the blood of the birds, because we simply could not afford the time to wait at some distance while each bird completed its death dance. And, at least early in the process, individuals in my crew, under some compulsion I could not identify, added to the chaos by trying to influence the movement of the bird, seeming to dance with it, further soiling their clothes. We could not find anyone who wanted to clean the clothes we wore. Thus, after the last bird was placed into the tub of hot water, we went to a water spigot next to the bakery, undressed to acceptable underneath wear, such as a bathing suit, and washed ourselves clean before redressing with suitable clothing. The old bloody clothes were placed in the trash, which was later burned. Eventually, others would dismantle the shelter. For days afterwards, long after Thanksgiving dinner had been completed, flies, despite the best attempts to control them, inhabited the site of the killings. But slowly the story of this contribution to the celebration of the season—birds, axe, blood, hot water, old clothes, flies—faded into individual memory banks, resurrection dependant upon another season, in another time.

****

An Audience

I had worked at the dairy for about one and one-half years. Although there were a couple of boys older than I, I had been there longer than anyone at the time of this assignment. The foreman and the hired adults had begun to trust me with ever increasing responsibilities. I was one of the few to be allowed to drive the tractor; I believe it was a Ford product. It could be difficult to operate because of its instability at high speeds. While it had two very large rear wheels on an axle at least five feet long, it had a much shorter front axle, with two much smaller wheels, about 18 inches in diameter. Hard turns at significant speed could result in a turnover. Consequently, it had a governor that kept the maximum speed to about fifteen miles per hour. I drove it several times a week on the dairy property pulling wagons of hay and other materials. Yet despite my unqualified self-satisfaction with mastery of this machine, and having the trust and respect of the adults, I was surprised by the chore I was given one day. I was to take the tractor and pull a load of cow manure to the football field, where work was underway to prepare the field for the coming football season. The field lay on the eastern edge of the main campus of the orphanage, just more than one mile east of the dairy down a major two-lane highway that connected Dallas to East Texas. The implications of this opportunity were quite obvious to me; there would be a number of people at the site, quite an audience, to see me drive up with the load.

The manure was collected at the western end of the dairy barn in which the cows were milked twice daily. Each milking, even though performed with the help of electric milkers, took close to three hours; up to seventy-five cows were involved. A lot of cow manure was deposited on the barn floor during those hours. We removed it with the aid of high-pressure water hoses, flushing it with the water through a small viaduct that carried the refuse out of the building and down the side of a small hill, where it collected. This is where three others and I gathered that morning to fill the wagon with manure. In short order the wagon was filled; I chose one of the others to accompany me with the load.

I drove along a dirt road, which curved from the manure pit south of the milking barn to the main entrance into the dairy, a short asphalt road that connected to the highway. Since it was a day in the middle of the week there was some traffic, but I pulled onto the highway without difficulty. Humming along at fifteen miles an hour, we set our sights on the buildings of the orphanage, which we could easily see in the distance. Actually humming is not the right descriptor. It was more the sound, if it can be imagined, of a washing machine containing large irregularly shaped metal objects on a fast wash cycle. It had always been thus, but I had not heard it before at this speed; it was very loud. The other boy was standing on the latch on the rear of the tractor to which the wagon was attached and holding onto the back of my seat; we could hardly hear each other as we talked. It was a beautiful day with clear skies, possibly late spring or early summer. I admit to having been a little nervous as the trip began; I had not been on a public road with a vehicle before. But I quickly found myself settled.

Shortly after I pulled onto the highway going east, a large dump truck going west passed us; the driver seemed concerned about something. He had his left arm out the window and was waving frantically at me, and clearly saying something with passion; of course, I didn't hear what he said and he passed too quickly for me even to get a clue as to what he was trying to communicate. Shortly thereafter, a car travelling in the same direction came by with the driver equally animated. Then from behind, a car pulled around us at considerable speed. I didn't notice the driver, but the hood of the car seemed quite dirty. I felt a jab on top of my left shoulder; it was the boy riding behind me. I turned slightly to my left to see what he wanted.

The wagon we used to carry the manure was about twelve feet long and four feet wide, and was equipped with a manure spreader. The front 9/10th of the wagon carried the manure, while the spreader itself occupied the most rear part of the wagon. It consisted of several curved arms, each about a foot long with a large spatula-shaped structure on the end of each arm. The arms were attached to a common rod, which extended the width of the wagon. This rod, once activated, was powered by the force of the rear axle of the wagon. Within limits, the greater the speed of the rear axle, the greater the speed, and thus the effect, of the spreader. It was designed so that when activated, the spreader was capable of throwing the manure several feet into the air above and on each side of the wagon. The floor of the wagon was sloped towards the rear, and thus towards the spreader; the spreader was fed by gravity, with help by one with a shovel, as the quantity in the wagon was reduced. The device that activated the spreader was a lever that was mounted vertically at the very front of the wagon, so the driver of the tractor could control the operation by reaching backwards from his seat.

There was a line of several cars behind us. The hood and windshield of the first car was covered with fresh cow manure; the air was dark with the stuff. Of course, I immediately pulled to the shoulder of the highway and brought the tractor to a stop. The cars behind us accelerated as soon as I pulled over. I could not see the people in the first car—the windows had a glare on them from the light of the sun, and the windshield was becoming hopelessly streaked as the driver had activated the wiper blades. I could see manure on the next three cars; we waved as they sped away. The fourth vehicle was a pickup truck driven by a fellow wearing a Stetson, or hat of similar design. He waved and said something I took to be supportive. We surveyed the situation and determined we had lost about 25 percent of the original load. We also determined the boy riding between the tractor and the wagon must have activated the spreader when he grabbed the lever briefly to keep his balance as we pulled onto the highway. After a few moments of additional discussion I decided not to go back and refill; there would be too much to explain. And besides, I had an audience waiting for me.

****

Stabbed

We had been putting silage into the silos at the dairy for several days. One had been completely filled and the second one was about half filled. This was dirty and monotonous work and several of the boys involved resented being on this job. They had put their time in working at the dairy or on the farm and simply did not want to be going through this effort again. Although they complained frequently to those of us working with them, often in uncivil language, they said nothing when the adults who were supervising us were present. Instead, in typical passive aggressive postures they simply "played" at working, often to the annoyance of others. On this day, there was one boy who was particularly annoying: the loser (our term for such a ne'er-do-well).

In some ways the loser, and others with a similar attitude, had a point, theoretically. At the orphanage, everyone had a specific chore, the challenge of which depended upon the age, size, and gender of the person. The girls worked in the kitchen, in the dining hall, in the laundry, and in Sunbeam Home with the preschool children. The boys had a variety of jobs: working at the dairy with the milking operation, working at the farm with cattle, mowing the lawns of the campus, working in the bakery and the commissary. Often the assignment was for a year or so, but when the tour was completed one rarely was reassigned to the previous job, unless it was requested. But there were times when everyone had to work together on a common project in order to get it completed in a required time. Baling hay and picking cotton were such chores, as was opening the summer camp on Lake Texoma. Additionally, putting up silage as feed for the dairy herd was another.

The process began with planting and harvesting sugar cane, the main staple. After the sugar cane was cut, it was hauled to the dairy and placed into a machine that ground it into a rough mulch. This was transferred mechanically to another machine where the mulch was mixed with a variety of substances depending upon the formula the dairy farmer wanted for his cows. We used cottonseed oil meal and some molasses. The concoction was then blown through metal pipes up to the entrance into the silo where it entered the flexible portion of the pipe and thence down onto the silo bed.

As the silage was distributed around the internal confines of the silo through a long flexible metal pipe, it needed to be leveled so it would be evenly packed. This required the boys to move the silage around from spot to spot using pitchforks. These forks were unique to this job. They were shaped similar to the ordinary pitchfork, except the prongs were slightly longer and somewhat slimmer, and the fork itself was several inches wider.

On this particular day, the loser was using his fork to irritate others in various ways: by pitching silage onto the space previously worked by another; by pitching silage so that it entered the open-topped, knee-length rubber boots of another; by just blindly pitching a forkful of silage over his shoulder without regard to where it would land; by generally behaving as "a poor, decayed, ingenious, foolish, rascally knave," to quote a famous Englishman of yore. Something untoward had to happen, and it did.

A forkful of silage thrown by the loser hit one of the boys in his face. He cursed, and pushed the loser down into the bed of silage from behind. The loser jumped up, faced his challenger, and pointed his fork directed at the other's mid body. I was the nearest to this rapidly developing ugly scene so I moved toward them and forcibly commanded that each was to stop. They momentarily froze, giving me the opportunity to move between them, and to tell them to take a break. After a brief moment of suspense, they seem to relax, and I did also. Then, the loser inexplicably lifted his fork, pointed it at the other boy who was turning away, and thrust it toward him. Reflexively, I raised my fork with one hand into the space between them, and with the other reached toward the thrusting fork.

I knew immediately from the intensity of the pain that I had suffered a serious injury to my hand. I let out an uncontrolled yelp, which froze everyone in place. There were five of us in the silo, now all silent and stone still. The loser was holding his fork, a prong of which had penetrated my hand through the glove I was wearing. The intended victim was looking at me with a mixture of horror and disbelief. The reactions of the others I did not observe; my attention was riveted on my right hand. I ordered the boy with the fork not to move as I took stock of the situation. He appeared to be on the verge of collapse: pale, eyes and mouth wide open, trembling. I asked one of the other boys to relieve the assailant of his fork and another one to go get the foreman. In the meantime, we waited.

Not visible to one outside was a vertical opening in the silo that extended from ground level to the dome of the silo. As one rose through the silo, this opening was broken by a series of crossing metal bars that served as a ladder. As the silo was filled with silage, the opening was progressively closed with wooden gates about two feet square attached to the metal bars. As the silo was emptied, the opening was recreated by removing the gates. The silage was removed by the use of pitchforks to throw it through the opening inside the dairy barn where it lay on the floor. It was picked up from the floor, placed into carts, and distributed to the feeding stalls to be consumed by the cows during each milking session. Access to the silage was obtained by using the series of metal bars as a ladder. This is the route by which help was sought and received.

The pain in my hand changed from its initial sharp and lancinating quality confined to my hand, to a duller, throbbing discomfort, which began to advance up my arm toward my elbow as we waited. Any movement of the fork by the holder brought a heightened and excruciating combination of both states. After what seemed an eternity, one of the supervising men arrived. He used a knife to remove my glove so he could examine my hand. The prong of the fork had penetrated the palm of my hand at a point between the base of my little finger and the wrist, closer to the finger. It had exited the other side about one half inch. After making sure the boy holding the fork was steady (everyone in the silo by this time was having trouble with composure), the dairyman went down from the silo to the tool room and brought back a large pair of wire/metal cutters and cut the prong so my hand was free from the fork. He then guided me as I descended from the silo, and walked to the office at the front of the dairy complex where he bandaged the hand, prong and all. He then explained what had happened to the foreman, who made a couple of telephone calls.

I was not listening as my hand was really hurting, a significant distraction. Ironically, this was not the first time I had been stabbed by a pitchfork putting up silage. One year earlier, I was working in the same silo when a boy accidentally stabbed me in the right foot while trying to scoop some silage out for the cows. I was wearing black, knee-high rubber boots. My foot was covered with silage as we worked, and he simply did not see it. Upon removing my boot I noticed a small amount of blood below the ankle. I wasn't wearing socks, but did not think much of it at the time. I finished my work schedule, went back to the orphanage for dinner, and went to bed at the usual time. I woke sometime in the early morning with a considerable amount of pain in my foot. I spent the rest of the night sitting on my bed trying to find a position for my foot that would ease the pain; nothing helped. When the others in the dorm began to stir and commence their usual morning schedules, I reported my problem to the adult overseeing our lives in the building. He arranged for me to go to the campus hospital where I spent a few days with a regular dosing of pills. I eventually recovered without any problems.

The foreman took me to an office in Dallas to see a bone specialist, and an x-ray was taken. The doctor told me the prong had pierced the bone in my hand, leaving a hole without actually breaking the bone. He washed the area and removed the piece of prong remaining in my hand with a grasping instrument he called forceps. He did not deaden my hand before he acted, explaining that to do so would temporarily cause as much or more pain as would be experienced during the simple maneuver he was going to make to remove the prong. I remarked afterwards that I was not sure he was correct, but I had had no previous experience with which to compare the current happenings. He bandaged my hand and gave me some pills. The doctor said he had not seen a similar case, so he recommended I refrain from strenuous work with the hand for two months. I was examined at the campus hospital a couple of times by a nurse; I do not recall any further problems with the injury. I was given the new job of daily taking our three breeding bulls at the dairy for walks lasting about an hour each through the pastures and along the small creek which ran through the property. Fortunately, none of them expressed interest in the occasional heifer we encountered.

Because the loser had a record of unacceptable behavior, over time he was eventually sent from the orphanage to live with relatives. My actions that day were characterized among the gossipers as brave, exhibiting leadership qualities, or stupid, certifying a need for custodial care; such is and has been the legacy of most of history's actors, especially minor ones.

****

Life Guard

In the summer before my senior year in high school, I was assigned caretaker of the community swimming pool on campus. I was responsible for keeping the pool and the dressing rooms clean and preparing them for use by the children according to a schedule that considered age and gender as reflected by the dorm in which they lived. The boys swam three days per week, as did the girls. I was also the lifeguard on the boys' day for swimming. The children swam for one hour, and then relinquished the pool to the next group of children who had appeared with their suits on and their towels over their shoulders within minutes of their allotted time. They waited patiently while the group before them finished and exited the pool.

The dressing rooms for the children were behind the east end of the gymnasium where we played basketball. They served also as the dressing rooms for the football teams during the season. The entrance to the boys' room faced north and that of the girls' faced south. There was a single wall separating the two rooms. For help, I solicited work from younger boys, aged ten to twelve years, and paid them for their work by allowing them extra time in the pool. While I retained responsibility for managing the content of chlorine and other chemicals in the water, they cleaned the dressing rooms after use by each group of children, replenished the footbaths, and hosed down the banks to the pool. The boys were very inquisitive about the activities of the girls, especially when they cleaned their locker room at the end of the day. Finding discarded elements of clothing was a moment of high excitement leading to much joking and fantasizing.

Once, I returned from a chore across campus and entered the boys' locker room. The door had been left ajar so my arrival was unnoticed by the three boys in the room; I sensed irregularity. Coming from the back of the area, near the wall that separated the two rooms was the sound of a small electric drill. As I paused to get my bearings and identify the activity, the drilling stopped, and one of the boys commented they were almost through. It became clear to me: the boys were drilling a hole through the wall that separated the two dressing rooms. Once I made my presence known, I was given the rest of the story. They had been paid by some of the older boys to carry out this chore. They were prepared to disguise the results so I would not know about it; such were the instructions from their co-conspirators. The damage was immediately repaired; I told the boys not to return the money.

The pool measured about thirty feet by fifteen feet, with the shallow end sloping to a final depth of twelve feet beneath the two diving boards, which were three feet and ten feet above the water. As lifeguard my main concern was that some of the children did not know how to swim. This concern was magnified by the fact that there might be as many as twenty-five to thirty children in the pool at once. With some of the younger children below twelve years of age, most near "drownings" materialized when poorly conditioned children, after vigorous play, had trouble standing in three feet of water. Resuscitation consisted of getting the child to stand up in the shallow end of the pool, and then helping him from the pool.

However, there were some who did not know how to swim and who were over eight years old. For these I had a self-imposed mandate to teach them to swim. I do not know from whence came this obsession, but it was there and I listened to it with a passion. Teaching each kid was not hard. With just a few individual and dedicated sessions with me, most learned to swim quickly. At least they swam good enough to take care of themselves in the pool, where they perfected their techniques on their own. But, there were a few, a very few, who were resistant to all instruction, whether it was rendered in measured and deliberate demonstration and encouragement or in terse and rough language incorporating the threat of lost swimming privileges.

At a point, I determined further instruction was futile. So I enticed the recalcitrant one, the one whose fear of the water had overtaken his sense of pride (the instruction was conducted in front of his peers in the pool), onto the lower diving board and threw him into the water. The immersion was always between the diving board and the nearest edge of the pool. Then I would jump in and talk him, as he yelled and flailed, to the edge of the pool. His arrival at the edge, associated with the cries of triumph from his peers, gave him all the courage he needed to accept success. Only once did this technique fail; I had to drag the poor soul to the edge of the pool. Needless to say, I was unable to get him on the diving board again. I simply left him alone to enjoy his swimming time as he wished.

****

A Birth

I had worked at the dairy for about one year. This meant helping to milk the cows twice daily, cleaning up the milking barn, feeding the cows, and bringing the cooled milk to the commissary, next to the kitchen and dining room. Twice a day meant starting at 2 a.m. and again at about 4 p.m. This was the summer schedule. During the school term only one or two of the oldest boys met the 2 a.m. appointment. The 4 p.m. milking occurred after school, so all boys assigned to the dairy participated. While we had mechanical milkers and adult supervision, much work had to be done by the boys.

Invariably the cows, with swollen udders, were waiting at the gate that led them to the milking barn when we arrived; we were transported to the dairy in the back of a pickup truck. After the animals were let into the barn where they found their way to the stall of their choice, we secured them for feeding. The cows knew the routine. As they pushed their heads through the gate at the end of the stall they had entered, we locked them individually with a secure retaining board against the neck so they could not advance or retreat. The space in front of them became a feeding trough, into which we placed a small amount of silage topped with a quart of cottonseed meal. This relaxed them until their time with the milkers. At that time, they were taken individually to a milking stall; there were three. The mechanical milkers were attached to the teats of the udders. As the milk was extracted it went immediately into the receiving cans which were kept cool until they were transported to the commissary on campus. After the machines were finished, we stripped each cow of the milk remaining by hand. Some of us became quite adept at aiming the milk at each other or the cats, or any suitable target.

The size of the herd ranged over time up to one hundred cows, with about three of four at any one time available to be milked; the majority were Holsteins. Once most of the herd had to be destroyed because of the presence of Bang's disease, an animal form of brucellosis. This is an infectious condition which may be transmitted to humans, hence the radical solution. The place was depressingly quiet for sometime, until the herd was replaced. This was my first encounter with talk of serious disease since the death of my baby sister in California. As then, I had trouble with the concept of loss due to invisible processes, or those outside our control.

One night as we started the early morning work, the foreman told another boy and me to come with him; a cow was in labor and was in trouble. We put on slickers and followed him out of the barn and into the south pasture, a distance of about one hundred yards or so, the erratic streaking of his flashlight sketching a path. He was carrying his work bag, which I knew held instruments and some drugs necessary to treat various problems he encountered in the field. It was quite cold and raining, had been for two days, and the ground was very muddy as we made our way along and across the paths the cows took on their way to the barn at milking time. We had rubber boots; mine were large. Welcomed at first, they soon became a liability; as we hiked they accumulated water because of the rain and became heavier and more loose, making walking a chore.

I heard her before I saw her. Her moans were low in volume but somewhat high-pitched, especially at the end of each expression. Clearly she was uncomfortable. I had witnessed births before, but they had seemed routine, nothing on which the foreman had made any special comments. But here he was troubled; I could hear it in his voice as he called soothingly to her. The rain was now harder and there was much thunder and lightning. We climbed a small hill, and then I saw her silhouetted by a flash of lightning to the south towards the main road, which connected the dairy with the orphanage one mile to the east. She was standing and looking towards us. It seemed as we approached her moans become more pleading in that they were more frequent with greater intensity.

On arriving at the spot where she stood, the foreman told us to stay back a few yards so as not to unsettle her while he made his initial examination. He walked slowly around her as we stood off, talking quietly to her. She turned her head to watch him but repeatedly looked back at us during the seconds it took him to complete his circle around her. As he approached her from the rear, he motioned us to come forward slowly and look. From the birth canal just beneath her tail I could see what looked like a large balloon extending out several inches. Within it, I could make out a small hoof. On closer inspection with the aid of the flashlight, I could see within the membranes what appeared to be a muzzle.

He told us the calf, being relatively large, was stuck by its shoulder, preventing the other front leg from coming forth. Since we had no other way to secure her in the open field, we were going to have to put her on her side and hold her there while he manipulated the front of the calf to free the shoulder and affect the delivery. Getting her down was not difficult. She was tired from the effort to that point, and did not resist a great deal. As we started, she was facing north. The other boy and I together pulled her by her tail toward the east. The foreman grabbed her head and twisted it as one would in bulldogging a steer in the rodeo, while at the same time pushing her to the east. Quickly she was lying on her right side. He told me to lie across her neck, keeping her nose free so she could breathe. The other boy lay across her hips holding on to her tail, keeping it twisted to maintain a good grip.

She struggled for a few moments, and the foreman entreated us to prevail; his language was not that of the teacher of agriculture in high school, which he was. Briefly I noticed his bag, which he had placed on the ground a few yards away. I knew there came a time in the life of a brood cow that the life of the calf was more important than that of the cow. I had heard stories from the older boys and from hired adults about such times, especially during difficult births. Decisions had to be made in a matter of minutes. Knowing what was in the bag, chillingly, I believed it was possible we were approaching that time with this cow. I talked to the cow to be easy, to be quiet, to be still, to let us help her with her baby, to live. Somehow this gave me more resolve to use all my strength to help hold her; as for the cow, I am sure she was listening to her own drummer.

The matter ended rather quickly. The foreman rapidly opened the membranes with his pocket knife. He stripped them from the calf's mouth and nostrils with one hand, and reached inside the birth canal along the neck of the calf, feeling, as he told us later, for the shoulder and the breeched front leg. As she struggled he beseeched us loudly to hold her tightly. I could see him straining as he pulled from within her birth canal with his left arm and twisted the calf's head with his right. Suddenly, his left hand appeared holding onto the leg by the hoof as he freed the shoulder. Immediately the calf began to slide forth, helped by the pull of the foreman now holding both front legs. The delivery was completed with a rush of blood from the placenta, which followed the calf onto the ground. At his command we released the cow; she just lay there for a moment or two. Then she slowly stood up and turned to inspect the calf. He took a piece of string of some kind from a small sack in his coat pocket and tied the umbilical cord, then cut it, separating the calf from the placenta.

The calf lay quietly where it fell upon delivery, forelimbs tucked under its upper body and face on the ground, exhausted by the ordeal. The foreman again wiped its face clearing the mouth and nostrils of the debris of birth. He told us to return to our jobs in the milking barn. As we walked down the small hill toward the barn I looked back a couple of times. He was standing motionless a few yards away from the two; the cow was showing considerable interest in the calf. Although the rain had lessened, the lightning seemed more active, but from a greater distance. Each flash briefly lit brightly the few white splotches of hair scattered within her black coat.

Over time I have often thought of that experience, especially when I have seen farmers on television trying to explain to reporters why they continue to farm and raise animals under the greatest of hardships: poor prices, floods, droughts, permanent exit of children from the farm. I know what the foreman did that awful night was not just a job. He carried with him to the field, in response to a calling of biblical clarity, the awesome power of life and death. Later that day when we arrived for the afternoon chores I found him in a small feeding corral watching the cow eat as her calf nursed. I saw no bag; it was as it should be in her small world.

The Fields

It was hot. Collecting hay during the summer was a job for all the boys in the orphanage who were at least thirteen years old, depending on their sizes. On this day I was working in the hay barn at the top of the "stack" of baled hay, my head inches away from the corrugated tin roof. There was little breeze, and I was sweating profusely. I had just descended to the floor of the barn to get some water when I saw a truck rapidly exit through the main gate of the compound and head toward the highway connecting the orphanage with Dallas. Within moments another truck arrived in the compound carrying several of the boys who had been working the fields; they had been brought to the compound for lunch. But strangely, they were excited, animated, obviously disturbed.

The orphanage was in a rural area of east Dallas County, about seven miles from the city of Dallas, surrounded by farms. The institution itself had one of the largest farming operations in the county, and the summer found most of the boys working in all aspects of the endeavor: milking, branding and dehorning, plowing, harvesting sugarcane for silage, shocking wheat, baling hay, picking cotton, building fences, and sitting around when it rained talking with the adults about life's promises and burdens.

Of all the chores, baling hay was the hardest. The crop was cut in the fields using mechanized equipment handled primarily by the adults. If one of the older boys expressed an interest in the more sophisticated equipment, he was readily taught to operate and maintain that farm machinery, a skill of value to some after they left the Home. The grass was usually Johnson or alfalfa. After it lay in the fields a few days to dry, it was raked into rows and then baled, each activity requiring separate machines. The bales of hay were rectangular in shape measuring about one by one and one half feet on the end and three feet in length, and were bound by two strands of wire, usually, or heavy twine. The final collection of the hay was simple. The hay bales were deposited individually by the baler on the ground in straight lines along the path of the machine, one every few yards. A truck was driven between two such lines of bales, with two boys walking on each side of the truck. Their job was to pick the individual bales up and throw them onto the flat bed of the truck. On the truck were several boys stacking the bales for transport to the barn. The stacks were usually five or six bales high. In order for the boys to get the bales on top of such a stack, the bales were initially stacked in the fashion of a staircase.

The bales placed on the truck by the boys on the ground were then handed up the staircase one boy to another until they reached the top. In the crowded confines of the truck bed, especially after a significant number of bales had been loaded, it took some thought and judgment on the part of the stackers to arrange the load so it ended with the truck properly loaded, with each bale secured by its position with regard to its neighbors. Although the bales were not very heavy, weighing less than fifty pounds each, alfalfa weighing more than Johnson grass, their size made them unwieldy, a problem if the boy did not use the proper technique. The most common method of handling the bale of hay during the stacking process was to grasp each wire with a gloved hand, position the bale by the wires so it was perpendicular to the ground, lift the bale up towards the chest using a knee for lifting help, and with a heave outwards and upwards, pitch the bale towards its intended target. Thus, the bale was placed on the truck and passed to successive levels in the stacking process. For final positioning, the boy at the top of the stack worked with a hay hook in one hand while grasping a wire with the free hand for control during the placement.

Once the hay reached the barn by truck, it was restacked in a similar fashion. On this day I was the boy at the top of the staircase, my head inches away from the tin roof so hot it could no doubt fry an egg. As I descended for some water I saw the truck leave, but I was so intent on getting to the water keg I initially took little notice of the arrival of the other truck with the boys from the field. But within moments I become aware of their excitement, and shortly thereafter the cause for it. I was told one of the boys had been either struck or run over by a truck collecting the hay, and was being taken to the hospital.

He was ten years old, small for his age, and covered with freckles. He should not have been in the fields, as he was too small to do any of the work. However, he was at the barn, no one knew why, and had asked the driver of the relief truck, the one that brought the boys in for lunch, if he could ride to the fields with him to pick up the boys; so I was told. When they arrived, it was determined the boys would not break for several more minutes— they wanted to finish the section of the field in which they were working so they could brag they had done more work than the other groups. When they finally stopped and started to board the relief truck, they noticed the small boy was not with them. Several boys went out into the field to look for him. They found him on the ground near the edge of the field which had just been cleared of hay, lying in what appeared to be a rut created by a large tire. He did not respond to the boys who found him; blood was coming from his right ear and his nose. The adults were quickly summoned; he was placed in the relief truck, and taken to a hospital in town.

I do not know what was done for him, but he died. He was buried in a cemetery near the Receiving Home, on a knoll overlooking the farm compound, after services in the church on the campus of the orphanage.

He apparently had no relatives who could provide otherwise for him. His was the only death of which I was aware during my eight years in the orphanage. I do not remember any talk about him or his accident in the days following the funeral, or since. I do not remember his name, or if I ever knew it. His was a life only he lived.

There is a conflicting report of the death of a young boy, during this time of which I write, allegedly hit by a car crossing Highway 80 (Bullock, 1993). This highway was a major road from Dallas to East Texas and divided the Buckner farm property. In order to get to the farm compound from the Buckner campus on foot this road had to be crossed. Another report from this time frame describes a boy falling from a pickup truck traveling between the dairy and the Home; he died (electronic communication, on file). It could be that of which I write is formatted by a perspicacity derived from the merger of two or more closely related memory data banks. I dwell on these somewhat different but compatible fact patterns because of the seriousness of the subject and the fact that there is significant variability in so tragic a story. This latter concern underscores the relative isolation in which the boy of my memory seemed to have lived. This seems a strange occurrence in an institution with so many children, but peer acceptance among children can be very fragile. I recall few victims of this phenomenon, but, sadly, there were a few.

SCHOOL DAYS and SUCH

The Home provided school for children from the first grade until high school graduation. Grammar, or elementary, school and junior high school were held in a building just south of the Chapel, and high school in a building on the north side of the Chapel. When I attended high school, it was a private school called Buckner Academy. In the 1940s, the school was part of the independent school system of Dallas County, but because of its isolation it admitted only children from the orphanage. However, in 1950, because of population growth, especially in density around the property of the orphanage, it was decreed that Buckner would have to admit children from off campus. This, the Baptist fathers were not prepared to do. The orphans could not be exposed to the lifestyle of those who did not live on campus. So the school system at the orphanage became private.

Most of the teachers were unmarried and lived on the campus during the school year in an apartment building, the Teacherage. I have no idea of their remuneration or benefits. I do know they were dedicated and well respected by the children. While they were certainly considered part of the Buckner family, there was little socializing outside of the classroom. Most also taught in the religious venues of our closed society. I recall few unpleasant interactions with any teacher; I do recall several very positive relationships. For the most part, I was a good student; perhaps that is a major reason for my memories. Several teachers stood out. In junior high school, geography class was a most pleasant experience because of the teacher, as was history. In high school I was particularly fond of my drama/speech teacher. And a science teacher who encouraged my interest in radio physics was very influential. A picture of our coach resides in my home office. But without question my favorite teacher was the high school teacher of mathematics.

✳✳✳✳✳✳✳✳✳

Irish Eyes

There is so much to be said about our high school mathematics teacher, truly a scholastic heroine, that any attempt to be comprehensive would be futile. So I will simply introduce her to you. She loved mathematics, but she loved teaching it more. And she did not just teach it, she insisted it be learned; there were no excuses for failure. I did not have a discussion with her about the following conclusions, but I am convinced she believed the Creator provided man with mathematics to understand why he was created, and how he was to behave.

Everyone in high school eventually came under her influence. While not every one enjoyed math as I did, she worked diligently and creatively in an attempt to make that happen. Her methods sometimes took us from the classroom to illustrate the practical elements of that which she wanted the student to know. I did discuss with her the appropriateness of taking time from the classroom for scavenger hunts. These were not, as I initially thought, games; they were practical lessons in applied geometry, which provided the basis for the clues to the hunts. Success in the project required problem solving by students working as teams. Once I looked beyond the classroom, and beyond high school, I grasped her thought, and retained it.

She never seemed to miss an opportunity to demonstrate practical applications of that which she was so passionate, regardless of the venue. Annually she left the classroom when summoned by coaches to help accurately place the lines on the football field and later on the running track. This need for her expertise was initially recognized by our coach during track season a few years before I began her classes. Once when our team competed in a track meet, mistakes in measuring the lanes, especially the staggered sections on the curves, led to near world record times in some events. She was most gracious in responding to the subsequent pleas for help, or so I was informed.

A redheaded Irish woman with bulging eyes and a probing stare, she exuded an intellectual passion which, combined with an intense personal desire that the student perform to his capacity, made her irresistible in the classroom and unforgettable as a person. These conclusions I support with two anecdotes.

My senior year another student and I needed trigonometry, a one-semester course, preparatory for college entrance. This course was taught every other year because of a lack of demand for it; it was not available to us in our senior year. But she agreed to hold the class for us during her daily assigned break time so we would have the credit. One other boy registered to take the course after it became known she was prepared to teach it. Consequently, I received my credit and she went without her daily break for the semester.

Annually, the school gave a medal to the student in high school for the most outstanding performance in a subject as judged by the faculty. She was the final arbiter of the math medal. I was given the medal three of my four years in high school, and was certainly prepared to receive a fourth one. But she demurred. Although she conceded I had the highest grade, she challenged me with her strong belief that this standard was not the sole criterion; there were other more important criteria for excellence. She felt I had serious problems with attitude and understanding the virtues of humility and graciousness. Among other sins, I was most intolerant of those who were less capable than I at solving problems in class, and who therefore "wasted" my time.

My disappointment in not receiving the medal faded by the next year when I won it for the second time. Apparently, I had corrected that which disturbed her. However, a substantial residue of the agony of disappointing her remains with me. Yet for some reason I never found the time to tell Mildred McCullough of her enormous influence on me as I undertook later challenges. Perhaps to have done so would have forced me to acknowledge publicly personal success, which I have never been able to do with comfort. Unlike an event in the sport of track and field, finality in the events of life is rarely achieved; it seems there is always a path leading onwards to another challenge. To stop along the way for self-centered congratulation is distracting.

✴✴✴✴✴✴✴✴✴

Hearts

Usually each class in high school as part of its homeroom activities would produce a play once a year. What complicated this custom in our school was that in the fall, and to some extent during the winter/spring calendar, the absence of the boys because of sports activities, especially football and basketball, made their participation with the girls problematic. On this occasion the boys in my junior class were called upon to put on a play involving only males. Earlier, the girls in the class had presented an all girl play while the boys were playing football in San Antonio. The titles of the plays are lost in the mists with which time shrouds memory.

In the story of the boys' play, I was an acknowledged overconfident womanizer, with little care for the feelings of the opposite sex. I hurt others through the vices of arrogance and self-gratification. I was a true misanthrope. My group of male friends determined to teach me a lesson, so they arranged for me to meet a girl from out of town who was virtuous, smart, very attractive, and was prepared to bring me to heel. The final scene was in the apartment of a male friend who was the cousin of the girl. At the appointed time, I arrived. She answered the door, and after a brief clarifying conversation in which she informed me he was not there and who she was, I convinced her to allow me to enter and to await his return. Wardrobe had performed an excellent job of makeup with the "girl"; at least the audience so reacted during the play, and later. The subsequent dialogue was advanced by me with one goal in mind, her seduction.

Eventually from the dialogue it was clear, however, she was getting inside my head; I was becoming the butt of her jokes and was losing control of the situation. Through the art of stagecraft, my friends, and thus their reactions, were visible to the audience from another part of the apartment; therein lay the value of the performance as both entertainment and as a morality play. The reputation of the character I played was destroyed as far as this group of friends was concerned. Toward the end of this final scene, I gained control enough to suggest to the girl that we dance. A phonograph was on the main table. I placed a 78 on it, we held each other at arm's length, and began to move in circles about the room. As the music advanced I added some twirls to the dance and, in a moment of terpsichorean exuberance, thrust her toward the audience.

With the rush of air under her long and rather full skirt as she flew toward the edge of the stage, the audience exploded. It seems he had chosen that day to wear as underwear a pair of loose, baggy boxer shorts decorated with large red hearts, a refuse from Valentine's Day, or some such celebration. So unplanned yet so opportune was the moment. The play ended a few minutes later. The actors were most pleased with the response of the audience, but clueless as to the basis for the terminal excitement until we mingled with the spectators after the curtain. No cameras recoded the sight, but years later during gatherings when stories of this kind are traditionally told, it was clear the memories of those who were in the audience were not shrouded by mists of any kind. Related during reminiscences was not only the substance of the play, but the innocence of the progressive nature of its theme; those were indeed simpler days.

$$**********$$

We Didn't

From *Webster's II Dictionary*, 3rd edition: tri-ni-tro-tol-u-ene. A yellow crystalline compound used chiefly as a high explosive: TNT. We had just made TNT! As we looked at it sitting in the flask over the Bunsen burner on the table in the high school chemistry laboratory, our thoughts were many, and disorganized. At least mine were, and I believed at the time my classmate's were because he was uncharacteristically silent. Finally, he murmured the obvious question: Did we really do it? Then from him came a low giggle, then a series of giggles. "What are we going to do?" came the follow up piercing question. We were by ourselves. It was late at night, around midnight, and we had let ourselves into the lab, on a lark, without permission. We did not know what damage could be done with our 30cc volume of mischief. We had not thought that far ahead. We had wanted to make it in chemistry class as a project, but the lab instructor, our science teacher, refused to permit it. Too risky he had pronounced. Not as bad as making nitroglycerine, but too bad for a high school lab. What were we going to do?

The classes in our high school were small; the popular ones might have twenty students. The teachers were dedicated, caring, and for the most part, skilled at teaching. Discipline was maintained by the practical fact that the school was a part of a bigger community of family. While most of the teachers were educated into their positions, some were there because of their backgrounds. So it was with our science teacher. He had been a radio operator in the U.S. Navy, and saw a considerable amount of the Pacific Ocean, and its ports, during and following the Second World War. Eventually, he met and married a young woman who helped him change his nefarious ways. Together they became employed at Buckner, where she taught drama and speech.

He had a gift for relating to the boys, especially the older ones. Often after school he would set with us on the Hill while waiting for his wife to finish up her after class chores; she helped publish the school newspaper. There on the Hill, a popular spot for the older boys to congregate, he often talked about the bad life he had before he met his wife, and the lessons he learned which he was dedicated to passing on to us. These sermons often included parables based on his activities and the human behavior he had seen in the Navy, particularly when on leave overseas in Hawaii and Australia, then in Asia. The narratives were graphic; he wanted us to be able to recognize sin before we embraced it. The narratives, if not the lessons, were later related and debated by members of his audience late into the evening.

He was a good teacher in that he kept the attention of the class. His strength was in physics, especially that of electronics. He taught from the book and was always well prepared to hold our attention with demonstrations and projects. It was obvious to me that he was less comfortable with chemistry, but the classes were always interesting. With this subject he often had some of us help him with a demonstration at the beginning of class, before the class as a whole went to work. The demonstration of the production of hydrogen from water was memorable. As we gathered around the table with the glassware in the center, he moved to light the gas flowing from the glass tubing, to demonstrate its presence; hydrogen burns. As the lighted match neared the mouth of the tubing there was a very loud noise, an explosion, with glass flying everywhere.

Although there were some minor cuts on exposed flesh, including arms and faces, fortunately no permanent harm occurred, even though only those with visual deficits were wearing eyeglasses. A couple of the students cried briefly from fright, and several went into short spells of uncontrollable laughter; my first experience with hysteria, or so he diagnosed. Later we found out the explosion had been captured by a tape recorder being used in a speech class on the first floor (our lab was on the second floor) ironically taught by his wife. He immediately called a nurse from the campus hospital to examine those with injuries. None required any treatment except cleansing with alcohol, then small brief bandages. Class was dismissed.

During the next class we discussed the lessons learned. First, he pronounced he should have satisfied himself that the demonstration was appropriate for the class, and that he truly knew the proper way to conduct the demonstration before he exposed it to the class. Second, we should all have been wearing glasses for protection. These were lessons from his military experience. Then some of us began to quiz him about other chemicals and explosives; we learned a great deal about military ordinance. We learned the difference between nitroglycerine and TNT. Thus, the birth of the idea to produce TNT, an idea he rejected without hesitation. I went to the library and consulted other chemistry books (there was no Internet). It would be easy to produce TNT; the necessary reagents were in the lab. After some thought and exploration, I devised a plan. I also convinced a classmate with a reputation as a risk taker on and off the football field to help me.

We would have to get into the lab after hours; this meant after dark. The lab was in a room on the second floor in the southeast corner of the high school. This was fortunate, because my reconnoitering revealed the outside light on the building at that corner was not lit at night, and had not been operative for some time. The construction of the building was ideal for the adventure. We needed to get into the building through a window on the second floor, as the first floor doors were locked and the windows had screens on them, which could not be opened from the outside; the second floor windows had no screens. The corners of the buildings on campus, including the high school, were constructed such that there was a ledge the width of the thickness of a brick every foot or so up the exterior to the gutters at the top of the building; the corners of the buildings were built-in "ladders."

The day of the adventure I cracked open the window closest to the corner before I left the lab. We met at the corner at about 11 p.m., climbed the "ladders" without incident, and entered through the window as if we had made a career of such activities. The preparation of the TNT was simple and quick. The only uncertainty was how much heat to apply to the flask to keep the contents liquid; if it cooled, it would become solid and more difficult to handle, so said the book.

What were we going to do? he asked me several times. I looked in the book, and got no answers. It was not a book for chemistry class. It described commercial uses for the substance, such as a detonator for minor explosions, without providing practical clues as to how to handle it. But it seemed the product was fine just as it was; it was very stable in its liquid form. Finally, there was a prolonged period of silence during which I reflected, and he paced. We had made the stuff, accomplished our mission. We had established no other goals. Sometimes heady accomplishments go unnoticed; history abounds of successes learned of later. With this thought I turned on the water to the sink, put on a glove we used in the lab for hot glassware, took the flask by its neck, and slowly poured the contents down the drain. He was motionless as he watched me. When the disposal was completed, I quickly cleaned the tabletop and the supplies, returning them and the reagents to their established locations. He simply stared at me without moving, or speaking. Silently, we left the room the way we came in, went to our dorm and rooms, and did not speak of the adventure for several days.

Eventually, one day without preamble, he asked if we had been in danger; could we have ruined the plumbing, or even blown up the school! The only answer, which we both took with us when we left the orphanage after graduation, was we didn't.

****

Victory?

I recall few times when I was punished, as I recall few instances of rebellion. As a preadolescent, I once had an ear twisted for talking in line on the way to Manna Hall, the communal dinning room. An effective discipline in school was wall sitting. One faced the class with the back towards the wall. After squatting until the knees were at ninety degrees with the thighs parallel to the floor, the back was pressed against the wall. The arms were in the lap. It was a favorite of the geography teacher, usually for talking without permission. But I managed to escape true corporal punishment, almost.

The genesis was innocent enough. As a sophomore in high school, I was a good, dependable student, whatever the challenge. In a production of the drama class, I was selected to play the part of the prodigal son in a modern version of the tale. The critical scene, where the son falls on his knees to ask forgiveness of his father, was not developing well. The emoting appeared embarrassingly contrived. I was self-conscious; I just was not able to make it believable. At first the students and the teacher were tolerant, understanding, supportive. That is the girls were. The boys were enjoying my discomfort, as only sophomore boys can. The girls, seeing that I was responding to the boys, eventually began to waver in their support, then they became downright negative. They chided me for not being independent, self-reliant. Then they began to mutter about courage, or the lack thereof. After one especially trying attempt, and critique, I responded to one of my critics with a brief but rather picturesque description of what I considered to be her upbringing, or of the deficiencies therein.

She responded with a firm, well placed slap across the left side of my face; she was right-handed. I responded in kind; I was also right-handed. The session ended immediately.

In a couple of days I was summoned to the principal's office and given a brief hearing, after which I was introduced to the disciplinarian. I knew him; he was our football coach. A rumor that he had played professional football was believable; he looked the part. The sentence was ten licks across the posterior with his "board of education," which looked similar to a ping-pong racquet but was twice the size in surface area and about half an inch thick. The genius of this form of punishment was that it was administered during the change of class when the halls were filled with students going to the rooms of their next courses. Despite the chaos created by their erratic flow, the students were quite aware of what was taking place in the principal's office with the door open and the building reverberating from the sounds of the board landing and the extracted vocal response. The final humiliation occurred when the student was sent out into the hall to find his way to class, a chastened, if not broken, young man. This adventure was never provided the girls.

I was told to assume the position, which meant I was to bend across the principal's desk and grab the opposite edge. If I resisted in any way, such as moving in order to avoid the swat, the sentence was modified to my disadvantage. And only the Lord could help if the back pockets of the pants were found to contain paper or cloth that might absorb the blows. The sentence began without delay once I was in position. Although never having been there I, nevertheless, was generally familiar with the procedure from reports of those who had. According to the male code contained within the word machismo, response was expressed in the negative: no pleas, no cries of anguish, no tears.

What does one do during this time? Does one experience flashbacks, as reported in near death experiences? Does one's mind go blank? How about prayer? The reports of others who had successfully taken this journey, and there were two brothers who had been on this trip several times, indicated the most successful distraction, or mind game, was to count the licks as they fell. So I counted: one, two, three, (survival is possible), four, five, (I think he is tiring), six, seven, eight (these three were further apart than the earlier ones), a pause, then nine. Another, longer, pause; I waited. Then I looked up; in a mirror mounted on the office wall I could see he was backing away. I think he is finished. And he miscounted!

"That was only nine, sir," I said as firmly and as controlled as I could; my voice had been changing for some time and I wanted to keep control of it.

I saw him stiffen, reposition himself, and draw his arm back for the finale. I had a very brief moment of satisfaction, even a sense of partial victory knowing that I had taken control. However, conjoined with that pleasure was the realization that the victory was Pyrrhic, a word I had, ironically, just recently learned. I heard it coming before it landed. There was a drawn out feathery whisper, perhaps last heard by Mr. Tell's son, distinctly separate from the following resounding whack, the tenth of the series. I experienced the force of the blow before the physical effect registered. The desk, large and rather heavily laden, bolted several inches toward the opposite wall propelled by my body as it absorbed the blow. Out of the corner of my eye I saw him immediately disappear into the inner reaches of the office through a door just to his left; he said nothing to me. The principal, who was in attendance, nodded to me, indicating I was free to go. Although full of students, the hall was strangely quiet. I briefly thought they must have known something unusual had happened. But no one said anything to me. I went, dry eyed, to my class, which was fortunately Study Hall. I wandered through the stacks for several minutes until I felt it was safe to sit.

I said nothing to anyone about what happened, but days later a friend asked if I had truly said what I said, "only nine". He had heard it from some one else. I spoke little of it, but it was clear from the treatment I received from peers that I had done something that resonated well with them. With time, I became aware of the source of the leak. Apparently the principal, who had little respect for the coach, told others of the incident, including teachers, who passed it along.

****

Homecoming

It occurred over a long weekend in October each year. The festive occasion began in the auditorium with a pep rally on Thursday afternoon. Its pace accelerated on Friday afternoon as the children, and alumni, prepared for the football game that evening on the campus. The bleachers and the scoreboard at the football field were liberally dressed in school colors, blue and gold. The coaches and the students prepared the field with white lines at ten-yard intervals and at the goal lines. The alumni began its enthusiastic contribution to the occasion with its attendance at the football game. The men paced the sidelines, exhorting the Hornets to feats of heroism en route to a hoped for victory. The women stayed in the bleachers and got reacquainted with former classmates. The cheerleaders were quite active in their full-length blue and gold dresses in leading various renditions of the school fight song: "Fight on Buckner Hornets." There was no queen or king of homecoming to present at halftime, nor was there a band to march. So the men took the occasion to play run and catch with the football, as in prior days, and in attempts to settle facts mutually disagreed upon, to play run and tackle. Limbs were tested; on more that one occasion several yielded, most being wrists and ankles.

On Saturday, the alumni wandered around the campus, some with relatives still in the Home, and visited previously occupied dorms and rooms, an activity that provided the more poignant memories. Light snacks with coffee and soft drinks were plentiful in Maris Welcome Center. Meals were served in an area above the kitchen overlooking the dining space in Manna Hall, for those who wished to dine with the children. The alumni were made to feel, and genuinely were, welcomed. This sentiment was joyously reinforced during church services on Sunday morning.

Of particular interest to my immediate friends and me was how old the average alumnus looked. We could not believe it. We knew older people looked and acted like the adults on the campus. But we had to face the reality that one of these days we as alumni would look like that. This idea was not only foremost in the minds of my peers and me as we observed the alumni from afar, it dominated conversation. Singled out, individual alumni were asked in not so subtle language how they felt about this phenomenon. Some laughed and acknowledged it, warning that it would happen to us. Others protested they did not know what we were talking about. In attempts to bring some understanding of reality by pointing out how unathletic they looked at halftime, we often found ourselves talking to the backs of their retreating bodies.

The year I was a junior, the drama teacher, with the encouragement of the school principal, decided to give the alumni a special treat. She was teaching a small class in public speaking. Because an early segment of the course focused on how to use a microphone in a radio station, she decided that we would put on a radio play. For the script, she assigned each of us to write a play of fifteen to twenty minutes duration; she would choose the one to be produced. It would be recorded on tape and played for the alumni in the auditorium. Following the presentation there would be a demonstration of the equipment and methods for the sound effects. At that time commercial radio shows were extremely popular; especially memorable were "Amos and Andy," "The Lone Ranger," "The Green Hornet," and "The Shadow Knows".

She made the announcement of the winning script by reading the chosen one in class; she chose mine. My theme was homecoming: Two alumni in their fifties met at the football game, not having seen each other since their class had graduated. I chose the game as the setting in order to maximize the use of sound effects during the broadcast of the play. They conversed of plans and hopes gone awry. One had been divorced, the other had lost a child to cancer. As the game progressed their respective positions worsened. The teacher became caught up in the emotional letting, and began to cry as she read. The principal refused to allow the play, if produced, to be presented; it was too unsettling for the occasion. The teacher refused to choose another and stalemate won. In retrospect, there probably was not enough time to produce it, given the need to locate the instruments for the sound effects and to perfect their use.

At the time, I looked upon the cancelled production metaphorically as representing an unfulfilling concept of homecoming, a concept I had learned from alumni who had participated. Not a small number of former students return after a lapse of several years, with certain expectations of class reunion and fellowship. What they experience is how different even their closest friends seem, and not just physically. Adults seem to be remolded by change faster and in more depth than are children. Expectations quickly yield to this reality. After a few minutes of cautious chatter quickly replaced by awkward minutes of searching through topics that have little mutual interest, the group slowly dissolves, the members retreating to the often mutually exclusive realities of the present. It seems that lofty expectations of a rewarding event, when confronting the unrealistic or unachievable demands of performance, succumb to that which is ultimately controlling—time, and change it brings.

BUCKNER HORNETS

At the high school level, the boys participated in organized athletics in three team sports: football, basketball, track and field; the girls participated in basketball. On relatively infrequent occasions, students were permitted to engage in individual sports such as swimming and diving and the boxing of Golden Gloves, high school division.

During my stay at the Home, the high school was registered in organizations for team competition. In the latter half of the 1940s the school was included in the Dallas Independent School System. The Buckner teams competed against public schools for team and individual honors. No students from outside the Home attended school at Buckner, so the district boundaries were drawn. However, at the turn of the decade as I entered high school, as previously noted, the Buckner officials withdrew the school from the public system. It became known as Buckner Academy, a private school, and entered an administrative organization known as the Southwest Academic League, in which its teams competed for district and state titles, and its athletes for individual titles.

Some of us who played on the high school basketball team also played with some of the adults in a church basketball league in Dallas. The most memorable times from that experience were the stops at a particular drive-in on Samuels Boulevard for ice cream sodas, courtesy the adults, after the games. The name of the establishment eludes me, but the girls who waited on the cars were dressed as Indian maidens, with feathers in their hair. We nicknamed the place Pocahontas. It was interesting to observe how adult flirting was carried out. But, this is about the kids.

****

Cheerleader

At Buckner there were few opportunities for siblings to get together, or even interact, except during visitations on Sunday when relatives came, or when they passed in the halls during school. There were too many kids and too few adults to watch them. One of the occasions when this could occur was at sports events. I played basketball. One evening we were playing a team from Texarkana, and we were beating them handily. I was having one of my best nights of the year. Every shot I took was going in, my favorite being a running right-handed hook shot. After my first successful shot, from out of the stands came a very loud high-pitched yell from Eva, my youngest sister in the orphanage, "That's my brother!"

I preferred basketball to football. It was cleaner, and in my mind more intellectual. Although preparing myself for college academically was my primary focus in school, I did harbor a tiny thought that perhaps I could play basketball in college. Prior graduates of Buckner had so been successful. Therefore, unlike my preparation for football and track, which was limited to the playing season, I worked extra in an attempt to improve my basketball skills.

As previously mentioned, during my last summer at Buckner I was given responsibility for the swimming pool. I maintained it during the swimming season, and served as lifeguard when the boys swam. In exchange for extra swim time, some of the smaller boys helped me with the pool. Their efforts gave me a great deal of free time to go next door and practice my basketball skills in the gym. I had no coach on site. I was on my own, utilizing what I could read in technical magazines as my guide. I was limited physically, I found out, as I tried to learn the moves of good players. I was not a good jumper; I never dunked a basketball, not even in practice. My left hand was useless to me except for the most rudimentary of basketball moves. I could not dribble between my legs; but I could hit the running right-handed hook shot, to the delight of my sister, Eva.

On the night of the Texarkana game, the small gymnasium was filled to capacity, as it was with each home game; it was very noisy. The score of the game mounted as we took a lead of more than twenty points. My shots continued to score. Each time, above the din, could be heard Eva declaring: "That's my brother!" Eventually, the crowd got into it. They began to yell, almost chant, "That's her brother!" with each successful shot, and with some not successful.

Retribution combined with revenge means getting even in a big way. A few weeks later, we were in Texarkana playing the same team. They had figured out how to guard me, preventing me from moving to my left with the hook shot and forcing me to the right where I was left with a less effective simple jump shot. They nicknamed me "brother"; their use of the term in their rendition of trash talk did not help my concentration. Our loss forced us to play and win another game, before we qualified for the state championship tournament, our route an example of how effective cheerleading can have unexpected outcomes.

✱✱✱✱✱✱✱✱✱

The Last Play

We settled into our defensive positions and postures; I was the right defensive tackle and he was at the right guard position. We were leading the game 7-6, the ball was on our one yard line, the game clock was running; this was to be the last play of the game. They did not have a dependable field goal kicker; he had missed an extra point, thus the score. I looked at the quarterback as they lined up over the ball; they were going to come at our position. The guard looked at me as we resumed our four point stances; he understood. The bleachers had emptied; everyone was on the sidelines at the goal line. Although we were on our home field, the noise was uniformly deafening across the field. The game was meaningless in that both teams had been eliminated from any chance of the district title. The final challenge of the evening simply came down to who was going to prevail on this last play...

In Texas, in the fall, Friday nights are for high school football. From the large metropolitan schools who consistently played for the state championships, and routinely supplied the colleges with their next stars, to the small town schools in West Texas, which supported six-man football, the lights were lit on Friday night for the game. At Buckner, we played the traditional game, even though we had to suit up almost every boy in high school to field a team. Although co-captain of the team, I was ambivalent about the sport. I was one of the larger players on the team, and in my senior year played several positions: tackle, end, linebacker, even a few downs as quarterback in an alumni game. The rules of substitution were such that each player had to play most of the game on both offense and defense. However, our talent was such we would have played that way regardless.

My ambivalence arose out of my concern for what was most important to me, which was my education. I was an academic leader in my class, but that was not enough. There was more to learn, and learning was the key to success. Football, with practice and games, including travel, was a distraction. Once, in my freshman year when I was sitting on the bench (I never played a down in a game that year), I was chastised for reading a copy of *National Geographic* during the game. Tellingly, I always had serious material to read on the bus when we traveled to games. And yet, it was necessary I played. While I received my share of honors when I played, I was most pleased receiving medals for the top grades in science and math during my high school years. But, I have become distracted.

Poised, seemingly frozen in time we waited for the play. Strangely, as I write, I perceive the pungent odor of the disturbed turf beneath us, memory acutely separating the freshly turned earth from the torn grass. Despite the chaos and noise from the sidelines and behind the goal posts, I heard the quarterback call the signals. As I recall the play, I see it clearly in slow motion. The players opposite us met us as we thrust ourselves across the line of scrimmage with the movement of the ball. The quarterback took the ball and moved back quickly from his center; there was no fake. He stepped to his right, then turned left toward his fullback who was on an angle directly at us; it was the most simple play in football. The opposing linemen had us occupied; I was being moved to my right and the guard to his left; a defining hole was being created. Inexplicably, the player blocking the guard collapsed to his knees, allowing the guard to enter the hole, whereupon he collided with the player blocking me, bringing both to the grass turf. I was free to move into the hole to meet the fullback. I hit him at the line of scrimmage with my right shoulder, wrapping him as tightly as I could with my arms, but feeling that he had more than met my challenge.

As I sensed defeat I felt a tremendous hit and surge from behind. Our guard had recovered and struck me with all the force he could. The three of us fell into the opposing backfield as the clock expired. For the briefest period of time I registered nothing, nothing except the smell of wet, stained, and sweat encrusted uniforms, the smell of the locker room after practice. Then we were literally lifted off the fullback and dragged toward our sidelines by the boys and men of the crowd. I had never experienced such joyous bedlam directed at me in my life, and never afterwards. The next week the school was buzzing for days about the last play. That was the reason for playing football on Friday night in Texas.

****

Disrobed

During my football playing days the need for certain rules which did not exist was obvious. For example, face masks were not required, and thus not used. I have a vivid memory of one of our senior football players, at halftime of a home game, lying quietly on a stretcher next to the south end of the team benches on the sidelines. On his face easily seen were the cleat marks of an opposing team member's rather large football shoe. Fortunately, no significant internal damage occurred. Substitution during the game was permitted sparingly. Thus, each player who started the game often played on both sides of the ball, foregoing the release of tension afforded by a return to the sidelines during change of possession of the ball. Therefore, if a player on offense felt he had been treated inappropriately by a member of the defense, he simply had to await change of possession of the ball to retaliate. Such was the case in a game, meaningless regarding titles, played one Friday night at the orphanage to close out the season.

I do not recall the opponent. It was a spirited game with players on both teams repeatedly admonished by the officiating crew because of excessive play, especially after the whistle. Of note was the play of a pair of brothers in our defensive backfield. While playing offense early in the game, one of them became incensed by a late hit. Both followed with the practice of routinely punctuating a play with a hit after the whistle. In addition, both participated in a lively version of the art of trash talking, before the practice acquired that name. The enthusiasm and energy with which they approached the players on the other team, and not just the player carrying the ball, was that displayed by the most dedicated of pest exterminators.

Our opponent had a small but swift halfback who had carried the ball with much success all evening, especially on sweeps of both end positions. He was too fast for our players; and he was tough. Regularly, instead of attempting to avoid the tackler, he lowered his head and met the tackler head on, including the brothers. In an attempt to control the problem, after halftime our coach moved me from my linebacker position to that of defensive left end. My primary responsibility was to confront any play that attempted to sweep my end of the line and to turn the player back into the center of the field where others had an opportunity to tackle him. After a few plays, during which the opponent's backs probed with limited success the center of our line, they called and executed a play requiring the halfback to sweep around my end.

I saw the play develop from the outset. As the back headed toward me, I crashed into the backfield unopposed, at an angle to tackle him for a big loss. It was the angle that was problematic. But it was his uniform that determined the outcome. The smaller backs wore pants that contained within them the pads for the hips. This created some protection without bulk, as they projected up and out from the waistline. As he sprinted toward me and, with a slight fake attempted to freeze me in my position, I sensed he was going to get around me. So in mid-sprint I dove toward him and grasped him by his pad with my left hand. I felt a blow to the left side of my face.

There was a merging of sight and sound and then I heard someone call my name, it seemed, from a distance. As I opened my eyes, a bewildering cacophony of lights from the field illuminators and the coach's flashlight greeted me. I was admonished to stay quiet and still, and at the same time to move my arms and legs. After a span of time indeterminate to me, during which I began to focus more clearly on my attendants and to answer questions about my well-being, I was able to stand with help and walk to the bench, trying to suppress a wave of nausea that accompanied me during the course of my trek. Strangely, I recorded no crowd presence. It seems as I tackled the back, his trailing heel struck me in the face, leaving me dazed, if not unconscious, for a few minutes. But, as I was to learn, I was not the immediate attraction.

When I grasped the ball carrier's uniform, his belt gave way and his pants were pulled to his knees by me as I fell. The pale skin of his backside coupled with the white of his athletic supporter served as a red cape to the brothers who were near. In a joint effort carried out with such efficiency one would be excused for believing they had practiced the maneuver, they began to complete the separation of the player from his pants. Subsequent reports chronicled varying degrees of success with observers and participants placing the pants, when last seen, at his ankles, completely removed and hidden behind our bench, or at stations in between. At this stage in the event I personally knew nothing of the struggle; I did not even know where I was.

The entire episode, from my tackle to the disrobing, happened in front of our bench and the bleachers that seated our supporters. According to others whose talents for observation I never had reason to doubt, a rather muscular skirmish developed between the two teams; I was temporarily ignored. While the disrobed player was trying to escape the clutches of our players, the rest of his team on the field either tried to shield him or register their disapproval of this turn of events on the nearest member of the Buckner team. The other team members who were on their benches across the field were intercepted as they made their way to the site of the melee. A few breached the virtual barrier created by the officials, but were only able to contribute to the relatively benign milling with pushing and shoving that existed by the time they arrived.

With control of the situation in hand, the officials huddled with the coaches for a few minutes, and declared the game over; we lost. At least that was what the official records for the season showed. Few on our team, uplifted by the overt support from the student body, which continued for days after the game, felt that to be the case. As for myself, the lingering headaches reminded me that in success there is often another story.

****

Challenge

He moved in front as he made the final turn toward the finish line, his stride smooth and confident, the balanced movement of his body that of the seasoned, mature runner. The spectators began to sense a result so unexpected that the words unbelievable and miracle became common among them. They were observing the finish of the two-mile run at the Southwest Conference Track and Field Championships in 1957, and he was not expected to be in this position. As I watched with his fiancée, a complex storm of emotions grew within me as rapidly as the distance to the finish line diminished: pride in the accomplishments of a friend, vindication for a rather remote challenge, a feeling of privilege at having the opportunity to observe a much revered human achievement. It began a little over four years previous...

The social event every year at Buckner was the Athletic Banquet where the individual athletes were honored. Each member of a team was invited to give recognition of participation, and each was encouraged to bring a date. This gave the adults an opportunity to teach the young people manners of eating in public, to be civil. The boys were brought together one evening, a few days before the banquet, and taught how to pin on a corsage and to seat the date, to use the various pieces of silverware, and to receive graciously any award won. The girls separately received similar social instructions. Those who did not participate on one of the teams were not invited; he was one of them.

He was one of my closest friends, and a rival for academic leadership in class, but he was not an athlete. I was one of a few sophomores who had won a letter, and after the banquet of that year, he was very troubled by the fact that he was not a participant. What could he do? he asked me one day shortly after the banquet. He was too short for basketball, and was small for football. While not overweight (no one was at the Home), he was however "soft"—he wore glasses and took piano lessons. Almost as an afterthought, and somewhat light-heartedly, I told him that next year we had no one running the mile in track and field. When he did not laugh or protest, I suggested he consider that event—a fourth place finish in the district meet would result in a letter. We consulted a book

I had on training for the various events in track. He talked to others, and quietly accepted the challenge.

All summer he was at the track running, lap after lap, usually after dinner but whenever his work responsibilities allowed. Several of us spent some time in the summer running at the track as a way of staying in shape, but we often treated such activity as a social event. Not him. He ran. Occasionally he would ask questions of some of the older boys about technique or strategy, and frequently I would run with him, my events being the quarter mile and the mile relay. But he did not socialize. We ran short distances for speed training, medium distances for pace, and longer distances for stamina. During the course of the summer I noticed two changes, subtle at first then quite apparent. He was improving in all categories and I was having trouble keeping up with him, especially in the longer distances. And his body was changing. He was no longer "soft." His legs began to slim, muscles became apparent. His chest became fuller. Often after a workout when I was glad to call it quits he seemed unaffected, fresh.

Then came fall and football season, followed by basketball. Outside the classroom, I did not see him much during those months; he was always running. Track season started slowly after basketball season for those athletes with skilled events such as the hurdles, pole vault, and discus. However, we held our first meet one week after the last basketball game for the pure runners, the sprinters and the distance runners. It was to be an exhibition event, not for the record, more warming up than commitment by the participants. No one informed him. There were five teams in attendance with competitors in every event including the mile. He won the event handily, beating the winner of the previous year's district title. He won almost every race he ran that year, including the state title. The next year, his senior year, was more of the same; he ran in the state meet with a flu-like illness and a temperature of 102 degrees F, and placed second. He won his letters and went to the banquet.

He went to the University of Texas on a modest academic scholarship, and presented himself unannounced to the track team as a walk-on. During his freshman year he began to run cross country and train seriously, with expert advice, in the mile and the two-mile events. He was declared the most improved athlete on the track team and was a member of the cross-country team that finished third in the NCAA national meet. For his efforts he was selected to run the two-mile event at the Southwest Conference Track and Field Championships his sophomore year.

The two-mile race began somewhat unexpectedly with him in fourth place after the first mile. The winner of the mile, who was expected to win the two-mile, and who was leading at this point, inexplicably dropped out of the race during the fifth lap. The two-mile title was now up for grabs. I looked at him as he found himself in second place. He realized the situation. I could see the change in his stride and his body movements as he negotiated the sixth lap; he knew his chances. As the runners finished the seventh lap, he took the lead, and control. Not just his legs were working, but also his mind; strategically, he was considering how to use his strength and stamina to finish successfully. The two runners immediately behind him obviously had similar thoughts; their efforts reflected such. They both challenged him on the backstretch of the eighth lap, but to no avail. He was not to be denied.

The track meet was held on the campus of the University of Texas. The crowd was not large but its partisan character became obvious, and it became more vocal as the runners entered the final curve before the homestretch. I told his fiancée I believed he was going to win; she could hardly hear. I had to repeat my words more than once. As he entered the homestretch I knew he was going to win; his stride was steady and even and his head and shoulders erect, the posture of a champion. Astoundingly, and yet vaguely anticlimactically, the distance between him and the other runners was increasing as he crossed the finish line. She and I hugged, both with tears, mine of joy and pride. I realized I had witnessed something truly remarkable that day, the successful culmination of a unique human experience, sought by most, attained by few. Gordon John Ratcliff had received and accepted a challenge for which he had no preparation. Then he proceeded to answer that challenge, prevailing beyond all expectation except, perhaps, his own. He was not only valedictorian of our graduating high school class, but also became its most accomplished athlete.

****

I Win!

At the orphanage there lived about 300 boys of school-age. Their daily routines involved school, work, and play. Organized sports, and sandlot softball played primarily by those also involved in organized sports, offered a few opportunities for individual recognition. However, for most, play was generally disorganized and void of the type of recognition received by the athletes. Thus, there was a constant search by the average adolescent boy for competition. And, to that boy whatever was discovered, no matter how transient or fleeting, had to define distinguishable accomplishments by the individual—had to define victory. Ad hoc games of horseshoes, washers, and marbles-in-the-round sprang up from time to time, depending on the season, the weather, and the availability of the sporting accoutrements, but never repressed the search for more.

As it was with all seasons, fall brought opportunities for a change in activities, and optimism. On the western acres of the property owned by the orphanage were groves of trees collectively known as the Woods. The older boys had unlimited access to these enclaves of nature; strolling through the Woods alone was a favorite pastime of mine. Because the Woods contained an abundance of pecan trees, in the fall, harvesting these hard shell pecans was a popular activity. The simplest way to harvest was to spread a white sheet under the tree, send a large piece of wood flying into the branches, and pick up the pecans that fell. Besides consuming them, we were able to sell some to small grocery stores along Samuels and Buckner boulevards. One day beneath the dark, shady branches of a pecan tree a game developed which would facilitate the search for identity by the players, a game consisting of a single, brief struggle following a challenge, and then unequivocal victory or defeat.

The pecan we harvested and sold to the stores was a difficult nut to crack. It was smaller than the soft shell pecan and as its name indicates, it was very hard. Since we did not have commercial nutcrackers, we learned how to crack the nuts by cupping two together in one's hand, and closing the hand tightly. In the tight space of the hand, the two pecans would be forced against each other as the grip increased, often reinforced by the other hand. Eventually, one nut would be shattered by the strength or hardness of the other. The meat of the pecan was tightly packed in its interstices and was very small in content, making the entire effort discouraging. Someone, perhaps looking for an alternative reason for the struggle, saw the result as one of a clear winner and loser. He therein decided to turn this activity into a contest.

One with a proven nut too hard to crack would challenge another's nut. The handler issuing the challenge held the competing pecans, and carried out the gripping maneuver until the resounding crack was heard, indicating the conclusion of the match. He would then open his hand revealing the results. The "trophy" was merely the knowledge that the prevailing handler possessed something the loser no longer had, a winner. The rules evolved rapidly, but not without some angst. For example, early on there was confusion and debate leading sometimes to serious disagreements over which pecan belonged to which handler after the fact, as they all looked quite similar. The serious promoters of this sport soon came up with a system of identification, and the body politic moved on.

The popularity of the sport expanded rapidly such that almost every boy from the eighth grade to the tenth participated, searching for the champion pecan. But as time went on that fall a disturbing development was noticed. A few, perhaps three or four, boys were beginning to win regularly. By this time, side wagers were being made. Little money was used as the boys had little. But items such as pictures with sporting themes and clothing such as caps were being wagered. Eventually a review by a couple of suspicious fellows revealed a pattern of behavior that seemed too odd to be coincidental. Each of the boys under review was always the challenger. If they were challenged, they never seemed to have their prized nuts with them. They never played unless they were the ones carrying out the event. In other words, their nuts never left their hands.

One day during a single event, the world of this competition unraveled with lightening speed. One of the boys under review had just carried out the contest. He opened his hand to reveal the all too familiar result; his pecan had prevailed. The other handler, without warning, grabbed the debris from the hand of the first including the prevailing pecan. Inspection revealed it was considerably heavier than the average pecan. Further inspection revealed the small hole that had been drilled into the pecan. After a rather frank discussion by all in attendance the pecan was placed on a sidewalk and smashed with a rock. It was filled with lead. How this was accomplished was never ascertained, but the sport died immediately and moved into the ether of lost ideas where it resided awaiting the opportunity for someone sometime in the future to ignite its resurrection.

Shortly thereafter the first snowfall occurred. The sport of bumper sledding developed overnight to fill the void left by the nutcracker experience. Boys would run into the street as a car passed, grab the rear bumper and squat, allowing the car to pull them as they slid along on their shoes, often two or more to the car. The contest was to see who could slide the farthest before becoming dislodged by the movement of the car, the sudden appearance of dry road during the slide, or fatigue. Thus continued the quest for sport, challenge, and victory, a constant search by adolescent males for ways to distinguish themselves in a society sadly lacking in such opportunities for so many.

HORMONES and PARLORS

Regular interactions among the children were abbreviated and controlled. Although there were no written rules that constrained the content and depth of interpersonal curiosity the children developed as they matured, strong rules that governed behavior were recognized by habit. Segregation, based upon age and gender, was well established and practiced. There were no proscriptions based upon racial considerations because there were no children of ethnic minorities at Buckner. Of interest is the fact the system of segregation, by gender and age, often resulted in siblings not living together. After my mother left her employment at Buckner, I rarely saw my siblings in a family setting. In some cases children became closer to friends their ages than with siblings. Not known is the impact this practice had on future relationships between and among siblings. As this chronicle will reveal, my siblings and I survived this problem, perhaps because of the bonding among us that developed during the early days of our stay when Mother worked at the Home and helped us to get settled.

The younger children mixed with children their ages in school, both secular and religious on Sunday, but only to the extent necessary for efficient management of the children. The older boys and girls in high school had more freedom. They sat together in class, and carried on conversations in the hall during change of class. On Saturday, they met at the vocational building to watch television in one of the few rooms on campus that contained one. On Sunday afternoon, a boy was permitted to visit his girlfriend in the parlor of her building, an event chaperoned by other couples sitting together in the parlor and by a matron of the building. Boys and girls were permitted to sit together in church Sunday evening, and the boy could escort the girl home to her building after church services.

There were few other occasions for togetherness because the opportunities were limited. Certain couples were chosen to decorate the large Christmas trees which were placed in Manna Hall and in the auditorium, providing the couples an opportunity to socialize in a traditional setting, that is without the ever present eye of an adult. The boys and girls did not have a way to regularly leave campus and have a date in the traditional sense of the 1950s; no one had access to a car for this purpose. However, as controlled and inhibited as the environment was for the developing adolescent and young teenage child, opportunities for testing one's evolving skills for interpersonal interactions existed if and when the child was ready to seize them.

****

Paralysis

She was petite, pretty with large pale blue eyes and near shoulder-length blond hair, and very popular. And she was ill. The doctors were not sure why she had lost the use of her legs earlier that summer after a "cold" with fever. She was taken to a hospital in town for tests, stayed a week, and returned to the small hospital on the campus of the orphanage for recovery. Heard was the word polio, but I did not know what that meant even though I was preparing to enter my senior year in high school in the fall. My summer responsibilities were to manage the swimming pool and serve as the lifeguard on the days the boys swam. Thus, I heard of her plight from some of the female lifeguards I met at the swimming pool. Although she had been in some of my classes during high school, we were not close friends, but had been friendly toward each other. I decided to visit her in the hospital, which was located on the girls' side of campus.

The first time I saw her I was shocked at how pale and sickly she appeared, and how distraught she was. She seemed glad to see me, yet she appeared very self- conscious of her state. The only treatment prescribed by the doctors was rest, and plenty of sun and fresh air. But the nurses were not taking her outside because the only wheelchair available was broken. This bothered me; in my limited experience, doctors were to be obeyed. Authoritatively, and without discussion, I picked up a chair from the nurses' station and took it to the front porch. I then went to her bedside and told her I was going to take her outside; I told the nurse to bring pillows and blankets. Without waiting for a response from either, I picked her up from the bed and started down the hall.

Her immediate reaction was to stiffen briefly, and then she relaxed. I was quite aware of one of her arms around my neck and the other one across my chest; they were so thin. Her head lay on my shoulder. I was most conscious of how light and fragile she seemed. As we proceeded down the hallway, one nurse scurried ahead to open the screen door; the other followed with a pillow and some blankets. On the porch I gently placed her on the chair, and the nurses arranged her gown and the bedding. Awkward moments followed. I asked if she was ok; she responded with a nervous giggle and a nod, blushing slightly. The tension created by my boldness evaporated rapidly; the nurses were particularly helpful at that moment by declaring how good this would be for her, and what a gentleman I was. I sat down on the steps just below her, and we started chatting. I do not have accurate recall of the conversation of that day, perhaps attesting to its impersonal content. After what seemed a very short time, I took her back to her bed and promised to return when I could, which I did often. Fortunately, the wheelchair was soon repaired, and I needed only to help her get in and out of it. I found it easier to talk with her as the days went by. We did not talk about her paralysis. Instead, we talked of the coming school year, plans following graduation, nothing deep or straining. Besides myself, she had many other visitors; and so the summer consumed itself.

In early August, we started practicing for the upcoming football season. It was more difficult to visit her during the day, and since boys were not routinely permitted access to the girls' side of campus after dusk, I saw her fewer times. One day I heard from the female lifeguards that she had recently started to move her feet; I had not seen her in some time. I went that day to the hospital. At my request she showed me the movement of her toes and her feet, and with her gown just above her knees, the movement in her thighs. Spontaneously we embraced for a few moments, and then release came with a slight sense of embarrassment for my display of affection in front of the nurse. I helped her into the wheelchair and rolled her out on to the porch where we watched the sunset, along with a group of her girlfriends who had come to visit her. Her subsequent recovery was rapid and she was back in the dormitory with the other senior girls as the fall school semester began.

On the Thursday before the first football game of the season the entire school—elementary, junior high, and high school—met in the auditorium for an introduction to the football team. As an elected co-captain of the team I was asked to make some general comments concerning the coming season. We were going to be better than last year; we might even win the district title. I talked about our first game. We had beaten the team last year 12-0, and I had no doubt we would win the game this Friday night, at home. On an impulse, I talked about her illness, and her courage, and then on behalf of the team, I dedicated the game to her.

We lost 30-0.

I am not sure when it occurred to me during the game we were going to lose, but at some point the game plan became secondary to me. What would she think? How could I face her, and the others in school? The last play of the game found me in on the tackle, on the far side of the field from the bleachers. I arose from the muddy ground—it had rained the night before—and started walking across the field towards the bleachers carrying my helmet. My thoughts were muddled, painful, dispirited; my dedication had been with such confidence, such bravado. How was I to deal with this? I had always been in control, or at least had support in which I was confident. But this was my problem, alone.

Looking toward the bleachers I initially could see little except vague forms of players and fans because the field lights were in my eyes. My path took me at a diagonal across the field toward the north end of the bleachers where the locker rooms were. After a disquieting moment or two, as I made my way across the field, into my vision approaching from the south end of the bleachers came two people. Initially, I gave little attention to them, as there was much milling of the crowd along the sidelines. But an instant later I realized she was there. Even before visual recognition, the awareness was signaled by an acute, intense feeling of anxiety in my chest coupled with a discomforting if not painful denial that disrupted my troubled thoughts. With a friend, she had sought me out.

I had repeatedly lettered in several sports, was academically accomplished, and had spoken often in public. Before that night people had talked of my future in science, the law, even the clergy. But at this moment I was totally unsettled, even frightened of the prospects of meeting her on the field, of having to say something. This was to be, I feared, more than awkward sympathy for an embarrassed young friend by another. At least I reacted as such. I could not face her. I quickened my pace and headed away from our intersecting pathways. The two girls changed their direction so we would meet. I broke into a jog, and they stopped. I looked fully into her face, illuminated by the field lights. She was disappointed; no, she appeared confused, hurt. As I reached the running track that surrounded the field and passed in front of the bleachers, inexplicably, I looked back toward them and caught a brief glimpse as they walked back toward the south end of the bleachers, to the girls' side of the campus. I felt sick.

All weekend I fretted. I had no one to talk to, no one with whom I could trust my thoughts. For the first time since I had acquired my campus "status," I realized I was alone; others with problems came to me, but I expected to handle my own. Of course, I was embarrassed we had lost; we had made the dedication meaningless. But it was more than that. During the dedication I had talked of her courage, and what we could gain as individuals from her example. That night on the field after the game I ran away from a difficult problem of my creation, which I didn't want to face; cowardice?

I dreaded Monday. We did not have classes together, but I knew I would meet her and her friends in the hall between classes. I did, between second and third periods. As she approached me on the way to the stairs to the second floor she smiled and said hello, while nodding and glancing ever so slightly away, a habit of hers I noticed when we talked during the summer, and walked on by, accompanied by two girlfriends; I do not recall their reactions except they were comparatively muted. Over time, as we encountered each other through the year I became more comfortable in her presence. Eventually she blended with the other students. I do not believe we spoke at graduation. A poet said "…regrets are few, too few to mention…," but some can be strong and lingering. I regret not giving her an opportunity to be gracious and, perhaps, reciprocally comforting and consoling. That is, and has been, on my mind.

****

Namesake

We were well-fed, clothed, housed, and schooled at Buckner Orphans Home. Lacking, for the normal development of children, were pets. Pets were looked for everywhere. Each dog that wondered on campus from the highways was treated like royalty. Invariably it would attract the attention of a group of boys, with the best of intentions. They brought food from Manna Hall, and old clothes for a bed located just outside but next to the building. And invariably, the dog was gone in a few days, wandering on down one of the highways. We named young cattle, knowing full well the steer was to be butchered for meat on the table. And we had Lassie from the films we saw on Friday night in the auditorium in the basement of the Chapel building.

We certainly had animals, and created "pets." Our work with farm animals— cattle, chickens, pigs—provided opportunities to make "pets." Certain animals were treated as pets: given names, provided with extra portions of feed, groomed. The genesis of this behavior is unclear, but we became almost obsessed with naming milking cows after girls we knew on campus, considering common attributes such as: appearance of legs, shape of nose, presence of long eyelashes, size and shape of hips, pattern of walking, tardiness to the milking barn, size of udders. It seemed by naming a cow after someone we knew we had acquired some interest in the cow, and we treated the cow as a pet.

We told the girls in school about the naming process, making it as honorific as we could, hoping to gain favor with them. In reality we used the process to comment on any characteristic of a girl that we could match with the cow, and vice versa, before we actually awarded the name. In fact, there was something exciting about discussing individual characteristics of the girls; application to the cow was secondary. What we did not consider in our search for the pet within the dairy herd was the possibility that the girl would actually see the cow named after her.

One day several girls came to the dairy on a home economics field trip, and to see their cows. Those of us who had not heard of the visit in time to join, in the back feed lots, those who had heard were left with the responsibility of introducing each girl to her namesake, if one existed. As we made the rounds with the girls and the teacher/ chaperone, the girls would ask about the named cow, and why the cow was named for the particular girl. At first we acted as if we knew nothing of that which they spoke. But the girls became more aggressive in their pursuit of the truth. So we began pointing out the cows, being as charitable and as lighthearted as the occasion would permit. With most of the cows no explanation for the comparison was necessary, and the reaction of the girl when introduced to the cow was predictable. This was especially the case when it came to the size of hips or udders, where the responses were uniformly negative, ranging from a nervous giggle to an unsuppressed gasp of shock.

After a few of these introductions were made, the rounds were abruptly terminated, and the girls left the dairy in the school bus by way of which they had arrived. The field trip occurred on Friday. Over the weekend it was rather chilly for some of the boys, especially when the boys asked the girls to sit with them during evening church services on Sunday. In fact there was an almost total boycott by the girls of all social activity, including the much treasured dating activity of parlor sitting on Sunday afternoon. However, with the start of school on Monday morning the girls had put the entire adventure into perspective, saw the humor, crude as it was, and all ended well. Naming continued, without much variation in the standards. After all, there was a great deal of fun enjoyed by all during discussions of comparisons. However, the endeavor remained within the environment of the cow; the boys sought and found other avenues into the hearts and minds of the girls, some questionable.

****

Violation

It was six in the morning and I was delivering newspapers to the adults on campus. As I had each morning since I had inherited the job, I picked the papers up at the substation, a facility on the north edge of the campus next to Highway 80, where they had been left for me. It was early spring, a slight nip in the air, a remnant of the mild winter. This morning I was being assisted by one of my close friends who, as he had put it to me, wanted to get a good start on the day.

After finishing the job on the north side of the campus we walked along the inner circular drive, which separated the main campus from a grassy area the size of a football field, in the center of which stood a bronze statue of the founder of the orphanage, bigger than life. As we approached the two buildings that housed the preteen and early teenage girls, Crouch and Buhrman dorms respectively, we separated. Unlike on the boys' side of the campus, we could not enter the girls' buildings but instead had to leave the papers outside next to the door of the main entrance to the building we visited. I headed to Buhrman, the dorm where the younger teenage girls lived. The lights I could see behind the drawn shades attested to the early morning industry of the inhabitants. After I placed a copy of the paper on the porch and turned to leave, my attention was drawn to one window in which the shades had not been lowered; also, the window was open. As I cleared a column framing the porch of the main entrance to the building I saw the window outlined in its entirety by the light from the room it displayed. It was then I saw her. She was standing, dressed only in her underwear.

The presence of open windows was not unusual, as security on campus at night had not been a problem. The orphanage retained a night watchman who made his rounds after dark on foot and in his pickup truck, a 1949/1950 (or so) Ford with a gearshift mounted to the floor. He was a strange little man, weighing perhaps 135 pounds. He was always unshaven , and wore a shabby long black coat. His duty ended each morning as the children made their ways to Manna Hall for breakfast. He often sat on a bench on the Hill—a very slight prominence near the high school on the boys' side of the campus—for some time after his nightly tour to talk with those of us who might be congregating there prior to the school day. He did not say much but would often allude to sights he had seen making rounds on the girls' side, which, as he put it, would drive us crazy, referring to the mindset of developing young teenage boys. No matter how enthusiastically he was pressed by his audience, I could not determine the truth of what he related as he was never very specific, just generically graphic. Perhaps, however, his stories formed the basis for my interest in the lighted windows.

I immediately recognized her; she was one of the prettiest girls in school. I stood transfixed watching her brush her short, blond hair. I recall no initial thoughts, except that my friend would appreciate a portion of this memorable moment. I saw him on the porch of Crouch dorm across the lawn; he appeared to be reading from the front page of one of the papers. Cupping my hands, in a stage whisper I called him. There was no response. Again I called, somewhat louder. Out of the corners of my eyes I saw her drop to the floor as if she had been shot. I immediately felt extremely uncomfortable and turned south toward the hospital to continue my route. As I briskly walked the one hundred yards or so, this discomfort I felt mounted. Indescribable initially, it turned to recognizable embarrassment, then to shame. What had I done?

I did not look forward to attending school that day; we would meet in the hall, no doubt. Most of the kids who knew me knew of my paper route. Who else would be there at that time of the morning? Would she make a connection? Although there was never a hint from her, much less a confrontation, when we did pass each other in the hall between classes that she suspected me, I remained troubled for some time. She was a very popular girl in school. At that moment perhaps she had been pleasantly engrossed in thoughts of planning her day, events to enjoy, people she was looking forward to meeting—a moment I had so rudely, so crudely violated.

Body Parts

I was always the smallest boy in my class until I was a sophomore in high school; I started growing that year and by graduation I was the tallest. It seems segments of my body grew at different rates. I grew up, not out. The sizes of my hands and feet lagged. When I was a senior, six feet and three inches tall, my shoe size was 8 ½ and my glove size was 7 ½, which explained the reason I could not grip a basketball with one hand. This latter statistic seemed to be of interest to several as I advanced through my career as a surgeon. Once, at the beginning of a medical conference, an anesthesiologist, in a spirited but good natured attempt to make my hand size an issue, inquired if all my body parts were so stunted. It took her some time to recover from what most thought was a very personal, even private inquiry.

In the orphanage, there was little privacy, but more as one grew older. The older boys lived two, at most three, to a room, with the occupants of two rooms sharing an intervening bathroom. However, in the dorms housing the younger boys, there might be four or more boys to a room, with all the occupants of a single floor sharing a single bathroom that had a single shower stall with as many as six or more individual showerheads without compartmentalization. Thus, several boys would be running around in the same state of nature at the same time. This invited comparisons. The younger the boys the less this was an issue, or at least, the less it was a public sport. However, with boys age ten to twelve years, comparison became a matter of culture. Comparisons regarding noses, stomachs, hips, and ears were part of the daily discourse in and out of the bathrooms of the dorms. But other body parts were not exempt. Of considerable interest among the males of this age, especially during shower time, was the body part, or member, unique to the male. And it was often the dominant subject as individuals took their turns through the shower.

However, as I passed through this age of the communal shower, the member was rarely the subject of ribald hilarity. This was because one very physically precocious boy was so dominant as to force all other comparisons to nullity. There were and are grown men without such prominence. Any one who chose inanely to compare himself to another only had to wait for the appearance of the endowed one to be brought to shame for having called attention to his relatively insignificant member. Thus, the chatter concerning this matter, if any on a given evening, was solely regarding when he would show, because of the spectacle. He often approached humming or whistling a popular tune. He was by nature a genial person; but he reveled in his notoriety. His entrance was flamboyant and formulistic. He arrived with his member fully awake, over which was draped his towel. The tune most often heard was that old hymn favorite, "Love lifted me."

With the older boys, such overt attention paid to one's member was just not done. Part of the reason for this reticence was the mutual expectation of and respect for individual privacy. Another major reason: the teenage male was interested in girls, not other males. Any suggestion to the contrary was a reason to exclude the boy from any accepted group of male bonding for interests incompatible with those of the group. This fact of life did not, however, prohibit all interest in male members by the older boys.

One day in my junior year in school I returned to my dorm from my job in the commissary. As I approached my room on the second floor, I noticed a gathering of boys before the open door across the hall from my room. They were quite animated, and at the same time were trying to control the sound that such a group invariably creates when intrigued. In keeping with the spirit of the moment I asked in a whisper, as I approached the group, what was going on. The group parted so I could see. One of the boys, a sophomore, was asleep on his bed without covers and clad only in his brief underwear. His member was fully awake and straining against his clothing, no doubt the result of a dream, the specific contents of which we would never be aware, but the general contents of which we were all aware. Someone declared it looked like a stone rod.

Thus was the instant birth of a nickname, which attached immediately and permanently. It was subsequently shortened to "Stoney," when it became difficult to explain to his female classmates the origin of the nickname; stoney was a reasonable description of his generally quiet, unflappable character. He was not thrilled with this acquisition, especially when it was used over the public address system in a basketball game or at a track meet. But to the day of graduation he was so addressed by all, a working tribute to our fascination with body parts.

****

The Desert

She lay among the rocks a few feet below me crying softly, no hysterics. I could see a small amount of blood on her forehead; I was also acutely aware of the startled and apprehensive looks of other climbers below me. I had told her she should not come any higher as the loafers she was wearing were not suited for the rocky and unstable ground she had to traverse. This day in the desert was to be different than I planned.

I love the desert. It seems I always have. Maybe this affair began when my father drove us to California from Texas; it certainly blossomed on this school trip, a reward for successfully completing a course on the life of Christ. The class was given in the sophomore year of high school and fifteen of us qualified for the trip. The trip was west to Carlsbad Caverns in New Mexico, to El Paso, and Alpine, then home through Ft. Stockton and San Angelo. It lasted about ten days.

The drive from Dallas into the desert of West Texas was filled with enchanting sights. I had not remembered being so captivated by landscape since the orange groves of California. The mornings were cool, the air crisp, the mountains so clear in relief they seemed touchable. In the afternoons, the muscular heat of the summer was stifling, even oppressive; but the scenery was gorgeous. The night before, our little caravan of three cars that carried four adults and us had checked into a motel at Marfa shortly before dinner.

The night we arrived in Marfa was one of those for which the adolescent mind, trying to determine what is relevant in its body's world, carves out a storage place of cavernous yet intimate proportions for memories. After dinner I spent hours in pillow talk on the telephone with one of the girls in the next room, the culmination of a day of innocent exploration regarding who we were and the nature of the world around us. Traversing the miles on the approach to Marfa, we had spent hours surreptitiously holding hands in the backseat of the station wagon in which we were riding, talking endlessly. The fact that she occasionally held the hand of the other occupant of the backseat was of little concern to me. Somehow I knew that something had to develop between her and me before I could concern myself about her and him. As my roommate that evening, he encouraged my interests, spending little time himself on the phone with her and her roommate; the evening was mine as were the memories stored.

According to this day's schedule, we were to explore the region by car and stop for a picnic lunch before continuing our trip. During the long drive the day before, we talked of climbing the hills. The hills we addressed, as we pulled off the road for lunch, were not those of the distant mountains but, rather, two piles of rough rocks extending several dozens of feet from the desert floor—loose rocks contained by tufts of dry, sticky brush; no cactus, just hard scrabble brush. The girls would stay with the chaperones and prepare lunch at a small spot a few yards from the side of the road; there were a couple of small trees for shade, and a picnic table under each. The boys would explore the desert and climb. None of us was dressed for the effort, but it didn't require much, so we thought. As we gathered after alighting from the cars, engaging in random chatter, I sensed a need to be alone on this adventure. Dawn had found me with much on my mind from the evening before.

To begin the climb, I headed up away from the group. The initial moments were mindless: a step here, the test of footing there, a glance across the valley through which the road ran. Having parted from the group first, there was no one above to distract me. I focused on a rather flat rock perhaps twenty-five yards away and above me as a suitable destination. But coincident with this decision I heard breathing; a look down revealed a girl from another car, who I did not know well despite having taken the course with her. She was a few yards below, struggling, having trouble with her balance, clearly winded. I called out, suggesting she return; she smiled, but ignored me. Twice I sat down, to encourage her to change her mind. She sat also, keeping her distance. I noticed what I took to be a more difficult approach up; surely she would be dissuaded. At first she was, then she seemed to accept the challenge. Go back, I (almost) pleaded. Her rejection was firm; she silently but vigorously shook her head and reached up with emphasis for a grip on the next rock. It dislodged and she collapsed backwards, tumbling headfirst over a rather large conical shaped stone, dissolving into a heap of blue (dress) and white (slip), her final position punctuated by an audible thump, accompanied by a brief puff of dust. No scream, just a faint explosive cry of pain, admixed with surprise.

In a few steps I was standing over her. I took her hand and encouraged her to stand; she couldn't or wouldn't. Others were converging. Somehow I felt responsible. Perhaps if I had not attempted to add difficulty to her efforts by the path I chose...perhaps if I had simply returned below... perhaps if I had made an effort to help her enjoy her efforts. I reached down, took her into my arms, lifted her to my chest, and started down the hill. My main concern as I responded to the offers of help from the first to arrive was my stability among the loose rocks as I descended; I needed room. Thus, without assistance I carried her down to the valley floor, where I was relieved of my burden by one of the male chaperones. He placed her in the middle seat of one of the station wagons, where he looked at her head briefly and asked her questions. He announced he was taking her to the hospital in Marfa to be seen by a doctor, but he felt she was going to be all right. I was not. It was very clear to me from the looks and whispers of all in attendance that I should and, thus, would accompany her to the hospital.

There, I was left alone. Another chaperone and a couple of girls went along and occupied her time while we waited for the doctor. He took a few minutes to clean her wound—no stitches were necessary—and then pronounce her ready to return to the picnic. The microcosm of teen culture in which I found myself immersed dictated that for the next twenty-four hours I pay attention to her and her concerns, which, however, rapidly included me less and less. Additionally, whatever spell was created through the magic of the telephone during that night in Marfa dissipated. When I finally returned to the backseat of the station wagon as we sped toward Dallas, there was no hand to hold. I was left to enjoy the beauty of the desert without distraction.

****

Steam Heat

Most of the buildings the children lived in were built in the 1930s. By the ecological standards of the 1950s most were noncompliant because of the presence of material such as asbestos. We knew nothing of this until years later for many reasons, the main one being it had no direct bearing on our lives as we were living them day to day. One interesting fact that did have a bearing to some was that the buildings were heated by steam that was generated in the power plant and transferred by pipe to the buildings. The pipes were in underground passageways that were big enough so a boy could make his way through the maze, to almost any building he wished. With the help of an accomplice in the building to open the door at the interface between passageway and building, the boy could visit any building any time, day or night. Those boys who had jobs at the power plant learned the map of the maze; those of us who did not have that job learned from those who did.

Regarding raising the children and indoctrinating them morally, it was telling that there were very few stories circulating about scandalous behavior between boys and girls, and even fewer that became scandals. On very rare occasions there was some talk among the older boys of the sudden disappearance of a girl, but always in the not so immediate past. There was one story that circulated briefly of a boy who left a year before he was due to graduate, and who returned occasionally at night to visit one of the girls in her dorm. This story seemed discredited when it became obvious that he would have to visit her in the presence of others in her dorm. On the other hand it did raise possibilities even more salacious. Similar stories were told involving the steam heat passageways, with the same obstacle—too little privacy—and the same options for consideration.

Other stories were more creditable, especially to those whose exploits added to the history, either as participants or observers. As the stories unfolded it seems the church steps were a good place for curious young couples to meet and experiment with their developing social appetites. These steps began on either side of the west entrance to the administration offices on the first floor of the Chapel. This building contained the auditorium in the basement, and the church on the second floor. The steps, between eight and ten feet wide, ascended directly from their origins for about one-half the distance to the second floor before continuing at right angle to their initial paths to end in a portico on the second floor. From here, one could turn east and enter the church, or view the statue of the founder, Father Buckner, and Maris Welcome Center beyond, toward the west. At the level where the stairs made their abrupt change in direction, there was on each side a smaller level space sized by the dimensions of the stairs. People who chose to sit on the portion of the stairs leading to the portico were unseen from the area of the campus surrounding the Chapel.

Thus, one evening I heard them before I saw them. It was mid-summer and I was walking west from some chore in the commissary that had occupied me after dinner that evening. It was after sunset but not yet dark. My path from the commissary took me west between the Manna Hall and the laundry, then along the south side of the Chapel. As I rounded the Chapel to turn north toward my building, Rupard dorm, I was startled but not alarmed by the voices, as they were not threatening in the least. In fact, the suppressed giggles and laughter were actually immediately intriguing. I stopped in my tracks. Intuition cautioned me to be wary. Ordinarily, such human sounds would be uplifting; they seemed out of place coming as they were from the south steps of the church; in fact, they were out of place. Listening for a few moments, I identified what seemed to be two girls and one boy engaged in some sort of fun.

I decided I must take a look, which I did by slowly climbing the first part of the stairs, staying close to the portion of the building on the left, which provided a wall for the stairs. My first view was spellbinding. The boy, without his shirt, was kneeling on a step with his back to me, clearly embracing a girl who was seated before him, her legs extended underneath him; the pattern of her hair from around his head strongly suggested they were kissing. The second girl was standing to his side. One hand was rubbing the back of his neck, the other disappeared in front of him, I presumed to his chest. From her emitted a suppressed but continuous giggle. Just as I completed the aforementioned observations, a brief move by him to change position resulted in the appearance of the first girl's face over his left shoulder; she saw me. Her eyes widened and she softly called his name; she exposed my position. He turned quickly as the second girl stepped away from him; I froze. He looked silently at me for a moment, addressed me by my last name, and suggested firmly that I should go to my building. I left straight away.

He was a senior, and they were twins from the freshman class. He later in a more private moment confronted me, and wanted to know what I saw, whom I had told, and answers to other questions I no longer recall. He confided in me that nothing went on except some "fooling around." He graduated. The next year the twins left, rumored to have taken a job looking after a rather successful elderly gentleman in Ft. Worth.

REFLECTIONS

I found in writing these tales, that some came to me more easily and quickly than others. I had to work extracting the details of the darker ones; the ones with good endings were more effortless, and the facts more certain. Perhaps this is the way the mind works, hesitant to relive that which has tormented it before. Once, when I recounted some of these stories to the enjoyment of most in a group, a psychiatrist— very seriously I came to determine—suggested that I should enter a prolonged period of psychotherapy. He believed the stories suggested I needed help in releasing the tension caused by their very weight. I suggested the process of writing did just that. The tales in this section I believe underscore that conclusion, and illustrate moments of insight or understanding of one or more important life struggles faced by a preadolescent child developing into the mid-teen years, while being raised by surrogates for a family he didn't have, helping to define the pathways he tread. Some were pathways broken fresh by me, but most simply traced ground successfully covered by others before me. In any case, I believe some help shape the basic components of my future decision making processes.

****

A Life's Pocket

At the Home we yielded much privacy on the main campus; I recaptured some of it by going to the Woods, a collection of trees of various kinds on Buckner property to the west. On one visit to the Woods when I was about twelve years old, I found a shallow cave in a small rocky hillock, with an entrance behind and partially concealed by a small grove of oak trees. Here I would come and sit and read and absorb the otherwise unseen events of nature. A veritable parade of animals would pass the cave as I occupied it: deer, rabbits, a fox, squirrels, many birds, and, once, a feral pig.

One day I was in the cave when I heard several squirrels chattering above me. Looking out and up from the mouth of the cave into the nearest tree I saw several of them quite busy, animated, at the crotch of a limb about ten feet from the ground. Curious, I waited until they left, and climbed the tree to see what the fuss was all about. I arrived at the spot in the tree previously occupied by the squirrels and at first did not see anything unusual. After some exploration I found a small hole in the tree opposite the limb I was on. I looked inside; it took a few minutes for my eyes to accommodate to the darkness. Eventually I was able to make out what looked like a nest, which was not as coarse as a bird's nest with its interlocking twigs. At the opposite side of the nest was a smooth, irregular shaped mass, darker than the rest of the nest.

Curious, I barely prodded it with a finger. It moved! I could see that it was a small animal about three inches long. It was a baby squirrel! Without another thought I reached in and lifted the squirrel from its bed and brought it out so I could get a good look in the fading sunlight. It was definitely a squirrel, and very immature. Its eyes were not opened.

Then I was hit with an uncomfortable moment of anxiety over what I had done. I had heard that once a baby animal was touched by humans, the parents would have nothing to do with the animal. That meant I would have to take it back to my dorm and raise it myself. What did I know about raising anything? I put him into my shirt pocket beneath the short Eisenhower-style jacket I wore, and headed home to the Home. As I retraced my steps to my dorm, my mind was racing: how was I going to raise this baby?

Of immediate concern was how I would feed him and where I would keep him. When I arrived at my room, without attracting the attention of my roommates, I opened my closet and placed the baby squirrel in the inside pocket of the jacket I wore to church and other gatherings that required a coat and tie. That evening at dinner I asked the girl who was waiting on our table what she thought. She immediately provided an answer and disappeared into the kitchen. She brought back a small bottle with a nipple that was used to "feed" baby dolls. It worked. The squirrel took to the nipple without difficulty; it thrived on the milk I obtained during my meals. In a matter of two to three days, its eyes opened. Then it began to crawl on the bed short distances. He was growing up! I named him Admiral Peabody. I do not recall why.

Admiral Peabody, or just Admiral, grew and developed in full view of everyone except those who did not wish to see him—the matrons of the buildings in which I lived. We were not allowed to keep an animal in the room, and should he have been discovered I would have had to dispose of him—I didn't know how as I knew no one who had gone through that experience. I recalled the boy who was trying to raise a bat. One afternoon while taking the requisite nap for the younger boys in the summer, he rolled over on the bat and smothered him. When the boy awoke the matron was making rounds and saw the dead bat before the boy did. In the resultant monologue, I learned enough to know Admiral would not have been welcomed should he have been discovered. He had his own shelter, an inside pocket in the nice coat I rarely wore. Uncannily, he always sensed trouble as the matron approached my closet because he would scurry from any part of the closet to the pocket when he heard her coming. He would not emerge until I came for him. As he grew I increased his diet to include the food that we received at our meals, and anything he got when he went to the trees.

I took him outside to play in the grass as often as I could. Soon he was climbing trees and returning to me when I called. The first time he did so was by accident. In the beginning, not knowing what his reaction would be when he first saw a tree, I watched over him carefully, and would not let him near a tree. One day while outside with him I was distracted. When I looked down for him, I saw him scampering to a small tree, into which he climbed without difficulty. He climbed cautiously at first, then with ever increasing speed, leaping from limb to limb with abandonment. For the moment I thought I had lost him. I sat on the grass below and watched. He halted in his assent, and appeared to be studying a bird's nest from a few feet away. Then slowly he moved toward it, obviously curious. Suddenly, a large dark bird flew through the tree, squawking loudly, passing very close to him, and exiting into a steep arc for another fly-by. Admiral's reaction was instantaneous and extremely focused. He darted down the tree at full speed, barely landing on the limbs he had used to enter the tree and, upon reaching the ground, came as fast as he could to me, and the pocket in my jacket. I never worried when he went to the trees after that.

He became a favorite of the other kids. They brought him food because they liked to watch him eat, often perched upon their shoulders, his dark eyes ever vigilant. He showed no favoritism, leaping from one shoulder to the next for the food. It seemed that as fast as he ingested the food he would emit the residue in the form of firm, dark, round pellets, which came continuously. In just a short time their volume if confined was significant. Thus, my closet required cleaning every day, because it was inspected by the matron regularly, but unannounced. His favorite treat was the crust of white bread adorned with a jelly of some sort. This particular food had attached to it a caution for the provider. On more than one occasion he, while eating, could not or would not define the interface between bread crust and finger, if the jelly were continuous across the border. Many of us were bitten without recognition of the event by Admiral; he kept on chewing. He was quiet; I recall little in the way of spontaneous chatter. He emitted a low volume continuous hum or purr when eating or when he was petted. However, when he was in the trees, and more noticeably if there were other squirrels around, he was as loud with his chatter as any.

With time I became bolder with his outings, and began taking him to school. The girls loved him, which brought a great deal of attention to me. Because of the interest he generated with the girls, a few teachers became aware of his presence. They commented on his cuteness, and indicated he was welcomed as long as there were no class disruptions. I made sure there were none. He slept in my pocket until I encouraged him to exit. He was extremely well-mannered when handled by the girls, wetting only on a couple, an act that lead to the usual mild display of hysteria. Encouraged by my success with Admiral, others looked for squirrels in the Woods and found them, including the East Texas version of the flying squirrel. These little animals created much excitement as they glided across the room in the dorm or over the lawn outside.

But no one seemed to have the success I had. Admiral and I had been together for two years when I took him on a trip to the dairy, for a reason I no longer recall. As I walked around the corrals where the bulls were kept he was perched on my shoulder as usual. One of the bulls was unusually active, snorting and pawing the ground, throwing up dust and debris from the straw that had been placed for bedding. Inexplicably and without warning Admiral leaped from my shoulder onto the top rail of the corral, ran down a supporting upright post and, then on the ground, toward the bull; he disappeared beneath the bull in the dust cloud. Two of my friends and I crawled into the corral after him. As we approached the bull he backed away, exposing Admiral's body; he had been crushed by the bull. There was nothing left to do but give him a proper burial. I found a box, and went to a segment of pasture near the creek underneath a weeping willow tree and buried him. Harboring no knowledge of animal deities, in a simple ceremony I conveyed his body and soul to whatever custody was available until we were united. I did not have another pet until I was twice my age at Admiral's death, and twice that before I again confronted the issue of animal spirituality.

****

I Quit

I spent the summer before I entered Buckner with an aunt who worked all day. I was left alone to entertain myself; I was nine years old. I found a friend who was twelve years old and, like me, left alone most of the day. He had a bicycle. Fortunately for me, his older brother's bicycle had been left behind when he left home to make his own way in the world. Before I met him I had no experience with the bicycle, and therefore he taught me to ride. The lessons needed were few as I was a quick learner. There were a few bumps along the way. Perhaps the most notorious, with the most significant impact upon the neighborhood, occurred in the garden of another neighbor who was very proud of the stand of bamboo she had encouraged to grow east of her house.

One day, not to far into my evolving relationship with the bicycle, I started down the street to the east of the bamboo stand, gliding down the sloping suburban thoroughfare, hanging onto the bicycle more than riding it. Initially I focused my attention on the front wheel, trying to keep it straight as my tutor recommended. He was trailing me by a few yards on his bicycle. Suddenly I heard him shout. I did not understand what he said but his tone reflected concern. Looking up I saw that I was heading towards an oncoming car I had not previously seen; it had appeared out of nowhere. I panicked and turned the bicycle hard to the right. In rapid succession I left the street, immediately entered the yard as there was no curb, and found myself guiding the bicycle toward the garden wherein stood the bamboo. I somehow maintained control of the bicycle enough to keep it upright and to guide it up to and through the stand of bamboo. Later estimates indicated I took out approximately 50 percent of the crop.

My friend avoided the garden, met me on the other side, and accompanied me as I crossed the front yard and entered the street in front of the house. Almost miraculously, I was in control of the bicycle and had no problems from that moment, successfully maneuvering it wherever I desired. There were discussions later among my aunt, my friend's mother, and the owner of the bamboo. My aunt never revealed the nature of those discussions, but hinted that such things were bound to happen when kids learned to ride bicycles.

We rode everywhere. We also developed a bad habit; we began to smoke cigarettes by imitating movie actors, and the old men who sat around on benches in front of the general merchandise store two blocks from my aunt's house. To begin with, we asked the men for a puff and they, laughingly, complied. Soon we wanted more than a puff, but we had little money, only enough for an occasional trip to the cinema with popcorn and cokes. My friend designed the solution. We would enter the store together and he would distract the owner with idle conversation while I took a package of cigarettes from the counter where they were kept unsecured. We each smoked about two cigarettes per day, puffing away without inhaling. Once I deliberately attempted to inhale; the subsequent rather painful spasm of coughing deleted that function from my repertoire of smoking skills. I learned to hold the cigarette with my lips and puff while riding the bicycle. Holding the smoke for a moment and then expelling it through my nose was an accomplishment applauded by the old men, much to my pride. I also mastered the technique of lighting the cigarette in the wind.

One day in late July, my friend and I took a bike ride to a lake about five miles from our neighborhood, smoking as we went. During the ride we consumed most of a fresh package of cigarettes. At the lake was a small store at which one could obtain fresh sandwiches, ice cream, soda, and other such foods, and we began our trip with that goal in mind. By the time we arrived I was beginning to feel quite ill. I had smoked more cigarettes during the ride than I had in any previous similar time frame. After a few minutes of rest, and a few bites of a sandwich, I felt so sick I did not know how I was going to get back home. And later I could not explain how I did. I never smoked another cigarette.

At the Home when I was a freshman in high school, a couple of the upperclassmen had qualified for the state meet in track and field competition. One of them chose to celebrate by smoking a cigarette underneath the bleachers at the football field. Given his standing among the younger athletes, he acquired much attention; his behavior suggested he thought his actions were to be applauded. He ran the quarter mile, an event in which I was beginning to participate; He asked me if this would become part of my training routine as well. My response was that at the age of nine I had been there, done that, and quit that. In truth at that age I had found smoking of no supporting or supportable value.

He chose at that moment to finish his smoke while declaring, rather defensively, I had much to learn. The truth was that we all had a lot to learn, about smoking. What I needed to know of the subject I had already learned. I did not confront this issue again while at Buckner.

****

The Debate

While we didn't need money for our necessities, it was nice to have some. Once a week we received five cents to place in the collection box in church and five cents for our personal use at the Campus Mart. This was supplemented by gifts from relatives who came to visit on Sunday. However, there were opportunities to make some money doing chores for the adults who lived on campus. By the summer of my junior year in high school, I had my driver's license and had captured the car washing business on campus.

It was an endeavor of some responsibility, if not importance. I was free to drive the car I was servicing anywhere I wanted on campus, and wave at whom I desired. Additionally, I could carry most anyone I wanted with me. My fee for the wash was fifty cents which included cleaning the hubcaps. After a few cars I came to realize I needed some help. Inspired, I "let" two or three of the younger boys ride with me and wash the car as I directed; I paid them five cents each. Because of my institutional job my time devoted to this one was limited, but I still managed to wash two or three cars per week.

It came to pass that I was asked to wash the car of a senior administrative secretary. It was a one-year-old Buick (I do not recall the model), cream colored, with four doors and standard shift mounted on the steering wheel shaft; it was quite dirty, especially on the inside. After picking up the keys from her I located the car on the inner circle drive parked in front of the Chapel. I drove around the circle twice, honking, and being silly; the younger boys, I believe there were three on this trip, enjoyed this display of nonsense, waving and making faces at those we encountered. Such was their need for entertainment.

The water we used to wash the cars came from a spigot located on the outer circle drive just south of the commissary building, next to the bakery. I drove from the inner circle to the outer circle on the south side of the campus in my usual state of self-awareness. The space previously occupied by the window, which had been rolled down, was now occupied by my left arm, with the short shirt sleeve rolled up, lending an air of coolness to the scene; the car was not air-conditioned. When we arrived at the washing site, the street was blocked by the commissary delivery truck. This truck was used primarily to take supplies from the commissary to the various buildings as they were requested; we had to wait a few minutes. This gave me time to explain to the younger help how to use the hose that was relatively heavy—and with water pressure could be challenging. Eventually, we were able to get to the site and wash the car. It took almost an hour; maintaining the focus of the helpers was how I earned my money. There were several distracting activities with the truck coming and going, food being delivered between the commissary and the kitchen, and the smells wafting over us from the bakery.

Finally, we finished, but could not leave immediately because the truck was again in the way being loaded for another run across campus. While we waited, I begged unsuccessfully for a cake from the bakery, and indulged in some lighthearted flirting with girls going to work in the laundry. In due time the truck was moved, and our way was clear to leave. We piled into the car with the boys in the backseat, careful to wipe our shoes clean and dry, and I started the engine. As I began to back into the street, I felt the collision before I heard it; someone had parked a small two-wheeled trash cart next to the passenger door of the car and I had struck it. Upon inspection I found a scrape in the door of the car about six inches long, just through the paint except at the point of initial impact where the scar was about half an inch deep. How was I to explain this to the owner?

I did not explain. In fact I did not speak to her. She had left the office temporarily, leaving the money for the job with another secretary. I went back to my room after paying the kids, sat on the bed and stared out the window. I couldn't explain it to her as she was not there, I reasoned. I could have told the secretary who gave me the money. But this was a private matter between the owner and me. I began to silently weigh my options. I could call her this afternoon before she left the office, but, she probably is not permitted to receive personal calls at work. I could tell her tomorrow; but, tomorrow is Saturday and she will not be in the office. By the time she got back Monday maybe she will think, if she sees it, that someone else did it. I have a responsibility to tell her what happened, and suffer the consequences. But, I may lose my business, and then the kids who I hire will not make any money. With classic Shakespearean complexity, the debate between the angel and the devil raged.

I had few responsibilities over that weekend; I spent most of the time reading and listening to the radio—the New York Giants lost to the Pittsburgh Pirates with Gordon McClendon broadcasting. He was the one who was announcing when Bobby Thompson hit his ninth inning home run, and the Giants won the National League title in 1951. But Thompson had the benefit of signals meant for the pitcher, Ralph Branca, signals which had been stolen during the course of the game. Fifty years later the discussions surrounding that confrontation were less about the home run and more about the stolen signals. What is the life span of a wrongful act?

Of course, after the weekend, I knew what to do. On Monday at noon I went to her office; she was alone. I told her what had happened. She was surprised, as she had not noticed it. We went outside for an inspection. I asked her what I could do. She said she had insurance and not to worry. Although the matter appeared to be closed at the curb, it seemed to me the last appropriate action was to escort her back to her office. The other secretary was present when we arrived and, seeing our glum faces, asked what happened. Before she could be answered, I apologized for the last of several times, and took my leave. Obviously, they talked about the event and how I had handled it because later that afternoon, while I was in my room, the dorm custodian came to me with a note that the other secretary wished to see me as soon as I had time; she wanted me to wash her car.

When I went over the next day to see her, she, as well as the owner of the Buick, were effusive in their comments on my handling of the event. Of course, they had no access to my debate with myself over the weekend. I guess what is important is not the debate itself but, rather, the outcome of that debate.

****

The Hunt

It was not that the rabbits were a nuisance; they weren't. But they were plentiful. They were no threat to our crops, mostly sugarcane for silage and Johnson grass and alfalfa for hay. And they posed no threat to the cotton crop, for it was grown merely so the boys, and some girls, could pick it to make money to take to the State Fair. No, the annual rabbit hunts were for sport. While most of the rabbits were the small cottontail some were the large and fast jackrabbits, which created the challenge because the hunt was not conducted with firearms. It was conducted with the use of clubs, the speed of the hunters, and an occasional dog.

Although there was nothing light-hearted about the killing, one dog injected some moments of amusement during one hunt in which I participated. He was a small greyhound, or whippet, absent his right front leg due to an accident the details of which I was not aware. He was quite swift, and regularly rapidly closed on a running rabbit. But, just as he was about to make contact with the rabbit it would swerve to another direction of flight. As the dog tried to follow he would go flying head over heels, because absent the leg he had no acute turning ability. He tried all afternoon on one hunt and never succeeded in catching a rabbit.

The preparation for the hunt was almost tribal. The experienced older boys would demonstrate to the younger, less experienced ones the techniques they had found useful in the past. They discussed strategy; maps of tactics were drawn in the dirt. The adults observed but did not participate. The basic technique of the hunt, and the kill, was for the boy to maneuver himself into the path of a fleeing rabbit and to strike it with a club he had prepared himself. The most popular club was one made from a broken bat used in baseball or softball. The bat was sawed off so the handle of the club was that portion of the bat that began to thicken just as it left the area of the batter's grip. The surface of the area of the hunter's grip was roughened, or covered with electric tape, to maximize control of the club. The club was used in three different ways, with variations.

The first technique was a throw that sent the club flying through the air as a missile, without spinning. This was accomplished by the use of a club with a rather heavy head, such as found in a softball bat. On occasion boys would drill holes in the end of the club and fill them with lead for added weight. The bat was thrown with a pitcher's motion, the arm coming from as far behind the boy as possible, whipping forward with the boy in a fully erect position, the upper body at thirty degrees turned toward the throwing arm, and the arm brought forward at forty-five degrees from the plane of the ground. At release, the arm was pointed straight ahead toward the rabbit with the wrist in a fixed, neutral position with respect to the long axis of the club. This throw was effective at a range of five to ten yards. Of course the metrics I have related above are approximations.

The second technique was a throw that sent the club spinning as a propeller. It came as a result of a side release, with the arm coming from as far behind the boy as possible, but carried forward parallel to the ground waist high. At the instant of release the thrower flipped his wrist outwards maximizing the spin. It was useful at distances up to fifteen yards; the killing zone was greater than with the previous technique because the entire length of the club was brought into play, not just the end. Although this technique gave a greater chance to hit the animal, it was not as lethal, as some force was lost in the spinning movement of the club. But it would wound the animal, allowing others to get to it and club it to death. This latter technique was the most successful of the three. If the hunter was able to actually strike the animal while holding the club, death was ensured.

The use of this technique depended upon the success of the strategy of the hunt. A field was located with the rabbits. It was usually one that had been freshly plowed, with the classic rows, but not yet prepared for planting. The broken stalks of the previous crop attracted the rabbits. The smaller boys would start at one end of the field in a line to flush the rabbits before them toward the opposite end of the field where the hunters were waiting. As the rabbits approached within the killing range of the weapons, the hunters engaged. The hunters using the above-described third technique waited for the animals to approach, running within the plowed rows. If the hunter were successful in his positioning, the rabbit's approach was such that the hunter had a clear shot similar to that of a golfer. A swing of the club as the animal attempted to break through the line was often successful in stopping the animal.

But the segment of the hunt that tested the hunters developed after the rabbits broke through the hunters' line. Success depended upon the speed of the hunter, his accurate judgment regarding the angle with which he attempted to cut the distance between himself and the targeted animal, and the accuracy of his throw. No rabbit was so slow the boy could actually run it down in a direct footrace unless it had previously been injured. Thus, it was important to accurately determine the angles of attack. With the first two techniques, it was unusual for a kill to be registered. If the animal were hit it usually required a direct clubbing for the coup de grâce.

This activity was not for the faint of heart. The only time I heard rabbits vocalize was in these hunts; during the final seconds of life they produced a high-pitched continuous scream, which was cut off by the final blow. I went on only two hunts, although they were held annually. While I practiced each of the techniques, I was never successful in hitting a rabbit. Once, I was positioned to catch with my hands a small rabbit as it fled the hunters behind it. I kneeled between two rows as the animal ran toward me. When it was two to three yards from me, my hands positioned as if I were a baseball catcher, a club thrown by another person struck the animal. The rabbit flew to one side of me, and the club flew over my head, barely grazing it. I immediately fell to the ground as a line of hunters ran past. I never knew who threw the club; I left the hunting field and never returned. The vision of the club, thrown with the second technique described above, has remained with me in clear detail. What also has remained with me is what I interpreted as the look of stark terror in the eyes of that rabbit.

****

From the Skies

The sound from above was foreign, different from any I had ever heard. A recurring, deep coughing, sputtering, discharge, it was a sound of trouble. Looking up from the back of the pickup truck, I could not see anything initially because of low hanging dark clouds, which threatened rain. Within seconds of the first sounds, however, I saw a large plane break through the clouds with smoke coming from one of its two engines. As soon as I saw the plane and the smoke, I noticed a small object fall from the plane, then another similar object, and another. At this instant the fall of the first was arrested by a billowing white sheet, which I immediately identified as a parachute, although I had never seen one except as a picture in a magazine. I counted: one, two, three, four… finally twelve parachutes. The plane continued over the horizon, I saw another parachute, then another, and then my attention reverted back to the earlier jumpers. The first was landing, and the chute was being rapidly blown by the surface winds toward the highway on which we were traveling.

The dairy foreman was driving the truck, and we were returning to the orphanage after completing the morning milking of the herd. He was one of several men hired by the orphanage to work the agriculture components of the operation. He also taught in the school system. Most of the men employed at the orphanage had military experience; it was less than a decade from the end of World War II. During my stay in the orphanage I developed good relationships with several of these men, and thus became exposed to the values that had sustained them during those days of strife and conflict.

The Dean of Boys, a robust gentleman about five feet six inches in height and about 150 pounds, had been in the Marine Corps. He was quiet, wasted few words, controlled with his eyes—his gaze the centerpiece of a disarming smile—and with his voice. With a rich baritone he commanded attention, led the singing in church, and taught the boys the basics of civility. Another gentleman, quiet and unassuming, was blown from a B-17 bomber over Germany, the only one in his plane to survive. He revived as he was falling, activated his parachute, and spent the final days of the war as a POW with burns about his body, especially his face and hands. With his wife, a very attractive and devoted young lady, he managed briefly one of the buildings at the orphanage, which housed boys in their early teens. There were other men with their own stories, some never told to us but never needing to be in order for us to benefit from lessons they would have conveyed. Our driver on this day was one of those men.

The surface winds were in control, and the foreman knew it. He told us later that he had previously seen the effects of high winds on parachute jumpers, and knew the potential for a deadly outcome. Complicating the problem was the fact the jumpers were landing in fields fenced with barbed wire. Several of the first jumpers we saw land had already been drawn into the clutches of the fences with, as we were to later learn, serious injuries. However, the jumper who had attracted our immediate attention was rapidly being blown toward and across the highway, having dropped clear of the fences. Suddenly, our truck accelerated toward the direction the jumper was being dragged. Several of the ten-gallon containers of milk turned over as the truck left the highway, and those of us who were not securely holding on at that moment were thrown to the floor of the truck where we rolled within the froth of churned cold spilt milk. Regaining our balance, we could see the young man desperately trying to protect himself by hanging onto the straps of the parachute. With a burst of speed the truck raced ahead of the dragged jumper; the driver drove onto the parachute and stopped, abbreviating the immediate plight of the parachutist.

As we jumped from the truck we could see the young man lying on his back, his face covered with blood. His eyes, wide open and moving rapidly and randomly, seemed searching for something, something stable, some haven of rationality, of calm. I do not recall any sound except that of his heavy breathing, and that of the unrestrained portion of the parachute in the wind. His clothes, once white, were torn and dirty. He wore what resembled street shoes, no boots. The foreman, placing his hand on the man's chest, spoke quietly to him, telling him not to move, that help would be there soon. With the first sound of the foreman's voice, the jumper focused his eyes briefly on him, then closed them, and seemed to sleep. He did not look older than our high school seniors. I was fascinated. I had seen blood on a human before, at football games, and once when two kids bloodied each other's nose during a dispute over a dog, but never of this magnitude. He lay so quietly he seemed not to notice us. I wondered: Did he not have pain? How could he ignore our presence? What had he just been through, and why? Who was he? What should we do?

We learned later the DC 3, or C 47 as the military version was called, crashed. There were two or three men killed; most of the rest suffered injuries from the parachute jumps they took. The one we aided was eventually taken away in an ambulance; I never learned his fate. It seems the majority of the men were being transported to a couple of military bases east of us on their way home on leave, the military term for vacation. They were sailors who had caught a free ride in the Air Force plane, in their traveling military navel uniforms, not prepared for this disaster. They had received a few minutes instruction on the parachute before boarding the plane at an airfield between Dallas and Ft. Worth. Within minutes after takeoff the trouble with the plane started and they were told to jump. None had jumped from a plane before, and the speed of the winds would have prohibited such a jump in peacetime training.

For weeks afterwards I thought intensively of that experience and the military. They were so young, not like the soldiers I had seen in comic books or the movies. I talked with our foreman about those who chose a life in the military. While he readily answered many of my questions and supported the decision of anyone to enter the military, he was most reluctant to talk about his military experience during the war, except to say it was a responsibility of citizenship, a concept to which I had briefly been exposed in school during civics class, but which became permanently imbedded in my person by the sight of the blooded face of the young sailor who had jumped into my life that day—a face defining patriotism. I carried that portrait with me during the twenty-seven years I spent in the U.S. Army Reserves.

****

Authority

I recall receiving little punishment while at the Home. Notable were a couple of times I had to sit on a rug in the middle of the parlor of a building without any distractions (eg. magazines, TV, etc.); each was a long two hours. In my sophomore year I received a paddling in the principal's office. My rap sheet was not very long, but it was about to get longer.

The orphanage was very well managed. The authorities prided themselves in keeping the campus clean and the children on time for events. This was especially true when it came to meals, as there were a large number of mouths to feed in a relatively short time. The children were placed in line and marched to Manna Hall from their buildings according to a schedule, a very tight schedule. The youngest girls, from Hardin dorm, entered the dining hall first, then the youngest boys, from Pires dorm. Thus it continued. The older boys came in groups, not in lines, but on schedule. I presume it was the same for the older girls; I do not know. With this schedule, eventually all (about 600 children and twenty-five to thirty adults) were seated. Following a prayer, all began to eat. A major job of the overseers was to maintain the schedule, as I was about to learn.

It had been a long trip back from a basketball game we played in Texarkana, Arkansas. Although we had won the game, the road had been long and the night short, and I did not want to get out of bed the next morning. I was still fatigued, I was not hungry, I had no specific chores to attend to prior to class, and I was in a foul mood. Our custodian came into the room as he always did each morning and, finding me still in bed, suggested I get up and get ready for the trip to breakfast; he then moved on to complete his rounds. I ignored his advice. A few minutes later, he was back. This time he was more forceful and direct. When I did not respond to his commands, he reached down and picked up one of my shoes. Concluding he was not preparing to put them on himself, and that he instead planned to use the shoe to punctuate his commands, I reached down and picked up the other. We stared at each other briefly, but conclusively, and then he dropped the shoe and left the room. I got up, having rethought my position on the matter.

A couple of days later I was invited to the office of the Dean of Boys. We discussed the event. He outlined the purpose of schedules and the importance of following them. He gave me examples, from the military and the civilian sectors, of this importance and the results, usually disastrous, when one fails to respect schedules. I sat there, listening to what he was saying, and absorbing it; I was trying to determine what my discipline would be. When he finally revealed it, I was initially sure I had misunderstood him. He told me that he was moving me back from Cullom into Rupard with the younger boys. Until I learned to act my age? No! I was being moved back to oversee the boys on the second floor. I was to become a house "mother," or matron, with all the rights and responsibilities of that position. And the move was to take place that day. I would be evaluated on the cleanliness and orderliness of the floor, the lack of tardiness by the boys to meals, to school, and to their chores, and the timeliness of my orders to the commissary for supplies. I was to be held responsible for the welfare of the boys and their overall behavior in the dorm and outside it. I would continue to go to school and to participate in sports, but I was in charge of the lives of the twenty-one boys on the second floor of Rupard dorm.

The term of office for this appointment was not revealed, but I was to keep my space in Cullom dorm; thus I did not have to move everything I owned to Rupard. Prior to the evening meal the first day, the Dean met with all the boys and me in the parlor of the dorm, as he had each time in the past when a new custodian was hired for one of the boys' floors. He handled this as routinely and as administratively as he had any such change involving adults in the past. He informed the boys I was totally in charge and had his backing one hundred percent, but told me later that excluded physical or corporal punishment. However, regardless of the formalities, everyone knew I was being punished, or at least had been given an opportunity to learn and to mend my aberrant ways. After his meeting I invited the boys upstairs to my room for a chat. I knew most of them for one reason or another. A couple played on the football and the basketball teams. A couple were well known for their lack of respect for authority, and I could see mischievousness welling in their eyes.

I was tested quickly. The first night someone sent a large metal trashcan rolling down the stairs, the noise increasing as it bounced from step to step. I heard the commotion, got up, and inspected the scene; it was about 2:45 a.m. There was no damage, but there was plenty of trash spilled from the can. As I looked into the adjacent rooms I saw nothing, heard nothing. This was odd; several boys from the first floor were roused and in the hall surveying the scene, but none from the second floor. A conspiracy, I concluded. I immediately went around the floor turning on all the lights and rousting everyone from bed. I required everyone to sweep and mop thoroughly every square inch of the second floor. There was a great deal of grumbling, but the talk given by the Dean at the outset took hold.

We settled in and the days passed. When I was in the building the door to my room was open until bedtime for anyone to enter for any reason. A popular reason was the radio which had been given me a year earlier by my mother during one of her Sunday afternoon visits. It was always tuned to a station with the latest popular music. The boys required so little to be entertained.

After that first night I took seriously my responsibilities. They had tested me, and I had prevailed. Demerits were given for minor infractions of the rules. An accumulation of demerits resulted in loss of privileges, privileges which included attending the movie in the auditorium on Friday night, visiting the TV theater in Danna Hall, the only place on campus that medium could be viewed, or trips to the Campus Mart of Saturday. On a couple of occasions during the first week after I found trash where it should not have been, the group was mobilized to again sweep and mop the entire floor. On the first day of the second week, the Dean made a surprise visit and found several of the beds not properly made and the furniture in rooms not properly placed. I wasn't there; he left me a note. That evening before bedtime, I shared its stated disappointment in me with the boys.

Sometime overnight a significant change in attitude occurred in the leaders of the group, or so I learned later. They decided the issue was not between them and me but, as always, between the leadership of the Home and them, and they included me with them. They saw an opportunity to make the situation a win-win for them and me and a loss for the administration. They reasoned that if the group of boys made their floor the outstanding one on campus, that would reflect on me and would illustrate my superiority over the other custodians. This is what happened. Unannounced inspections revealed perfectly made beds and arranged closets containing the boys' clothes. Every nook and cranny was spotless. The boys went to meals together as a group; they didn't straggle in. If there had been an award I, on behalf of the floor, would have won.

As it was, after three weeks, I was suddenly relieved of my duties and returned to my dorm. Responsibilities for the boys reverted to the lady who managed the first floor. In addition to her duties as housemother for Rupard dorm, she cut the hair of most of the boys on campus; the older boys cut each other's hair, the short flat-top the most popular style during my last two years in high school. She was a most robust individual with an enormous bosom, against which she would trap the head of a fidgety young boy as she attempted to cut his hair.

There was no exit interview; none was needed. I had spent most of the three weeks pondering my situation. I had looked at the world from the custodians' perspectives. I felt the weight of deciding for a group rather than just for myself. I knew the boys viewed me differently than they viewed the adult custodians; I was in reality one of them. And they gave me a break. Nevertheless, the view from my tower of relative isolation (I did have a private room and bathroom that I did not have to share) allowed me a glimpse of the responsibility and the loneliness of authority. It was an experience acquired with some inconvenience, but no pain. As I began to congratulate myself for surviving the challenge, I realized it was not about me at all. It was about the Dean and his wisdom in forcing me to address an abstract concept of responsibility through a pragmatic trial of work ethic rather than through an experience of meaningless unfocused discipline. He opened the door of my future for me.

****

Random Notes

One of the significant opportunities available to every child, but accepted by few, was that of learning to play the piano. My sister Anne took advantage of this opportunity and benefited greatly. I had such an opportunity and let it pass. I started lessons in the music hall located in the high school, in the seventh grade. The teacher was dedicated and patient, but I wasn't. She held personal instruction once per week, then assigned work to be practiced until the next instruction. Although the exercises introduced me to music in an organized way, especially classical music which I came to enjoy very much, I was never a good student of the piano. I practiced so that I could get through the instructions satisfactorily, but I was easily distracted. In the summer I regularly skipped practice to play softball on a field adjacent to the high school, often crawling out the window of the practice room on the second floor and climbing down the wall of the building using the brick "ladders" (see We Didn't). In my first public recital, I walked off the stage without completing the piece, simply because I didn't want to be there. In my freshman year in high school I injured the "pinky" on my left hand in football causing it to be permanently deformed, reducing my reach across the keys to less than an octave. My teacher challenged me: would it be piano or football? I chose the latter; she accepted my decision. I now wish she had not.

Sources of professional entertainment were few in the Home; we did have movies weekly and subsequently, television. There were few standard radios available to us; my mother gave me one, but most were not so fortunate. As an alternative, crystal radios existed. They were made from wood and wire, and required no electricity because of the diode of zincite, a crystallized mineral that permitted acquisition of the radio signal. This substance was rather expensive to obtain. After I completed chemistry in high school, I obtained permission from the teacher to make the basic substance, zinc oxide, in the laboratory, which I did. I sold it to the other boys for much less than the zincite cost, my first lesson in business. Although my product worked, it was not structured as the mineral variety. It crumbled rather easily, resulting in a life span much less than that of the mineral, a fault for which I had no solution; the customers complained—another business lesson. As a result of the third lesson--- that engineered obsolescence was not popular--- I closed my business.

But I did not lose my interest in radio. Our science teacher had been a radio operator in the Navy, and did his best to interest anyone he could in the subject of electronics generally, and radio specifically. I became enamored with the subject listening to the short wave radio he set up in the laboratory, and using Morse Code to talk to people halfway around the world. So I began studying under his direction. I eventually obtained with his help and support a ham radio license, WN5GBU. I spent hours on the net. Several other students and I, studying outside of school, designed and built, with his direction, a 1000 W transmitter. It was eventually activated for broadcast of church services to those confined to their buildings because of illness. Unfortunately, when I left Buckner and entered college, I did not have the time or money to continue this interest, a loss felt to this day.

Although there were no black children in the Home while I lived there, the music of Steven Foster was quite popular, especially among some of the adults, including the Dean of Boys. As a result, high school students put on a Negro Minstrel each year, complete with black faced subjects and white plantation owners. It was an extremely popular production, presented in the auditorium for all who could come to see it. I was not a good singer although I had a "rich" bass voice; I never had a major singing role. However, I did one year play the part of a black preacher attired in a frock coat and white gloves. Utilizing my vocal attributes to the extreme, I gave a sermon with all the passion, the gyrations, and the pulpit pounding that stereotyping could generate. It was politely received but I do not recall it being especially memorable. It certainly did not prepare me for the multiracial society I was to meet upon leaving the Home.

****

Only One

There is a reason this book is written in the first person. It is very illustrative of my life at Buckner. Although I had a few friends, some at the time quite close, I am rarely mentioned in stories about the Home in other publications written during my stay, and afterwards. Rare is the photograph of activity at the Home in which I can be identified, except in the obligatory portrait genre. I was never elected to a class office. I grew up in a world populated by me. I can only surmise the geneses of this reference point were the demands of my father as he left that I help Mother with the family and the entreaties of my mother that I must succeed, for the family. That is why most of the tales are about me and my vision of the world in which I lived, with the other characters, easily described without identities, in supporting roles; I allowed no one an opportunity to distract me from the goals given me by my parents, especially my mother. To some extent, others around me responded by giving me my space, as it were. I was never the target of jokes, nor was I sought out to participate in moments of frivolity at the expense of others.

An anecdote perhaps sums up this state of affairs tellingly. The position of valedictorian was very hotly contested down to the final week in school among three students, myself including. One day the announcement was made over the school's public address system. I came in second—the difference was very close. In my class period when the announcement was made the cheering was such that to this day I do not know if the cheers were because of the person who was named first in the class or because I did not receive the distinction.

When I left the Home the morning after graduation, I do not recall telling anyone goodbye. Yet I have no regrets related to interpersonal relationships while there. And, without applying judgment as to the correctness of the way I conducted my life's work, this experience in the Home of which I now write perhaps was a template for my future.

During my last year in school at the Home I did became friends with a girl one year behind me. She was the sister of a classmate of mine. She was the leading basketball player on the girls' team, and we often were together on the bus ride to play a game, talking with the coaches. Following graduation from Buckner I enrolled at the University of Texas, along with three others in my class; we came back to visit at the Home frequently. I had no other friends or close acquaintances at college to occupy my free time. With these visits, my relationship with Virginia blossomed; it was noticed by others when she invited me to attend class with her during visits. Following graduation she entered a school of Radiological Technology. Subsequently we married, and she became the mother of our five children.

CLOSURE

While the high school was in the public school system, it required sixteen units to graduate, with 0.5 units awarded for each semester of instruction per course. After the school became private, for reasons I never understood, the administration decreed that twenty units were required, even though the state still only required sixteen. That fifth year was called the academy year—the students were Academy Seniors. I avoided the fifth year by taking extra courses during the school years and during two summers, ending with 21.5 units. The administration of the Home, during each student's final year, searched on behalf of the student opportunities for post graduation education or employment, and housing. In so doing they called liberally upon contacts within the Baptist community and were highly successful. Every student in my class of twenty-one benefited by this effort. At graduation each student had a job or a place in school, and a place to live.

As for myself, I was nominated for a four-year scholarship to the University of Texas in Austin, awarded annually to the most deserving graduating boy in the high schools of Dallas County, based on criteria which included academic accomplishments, athletic participation, and civic engagements. It was the first year Buckner was asked to participate, and I won the scholarship. The morning after I graduated from Buckner Academy, I left the Home with twenty dollars in my pocket given to me by the Home administration. I, with the help of my mother, arranged to spend the summer of 1955 living with my uncle and aunt who were raising my sister Paula. My uncle obtained a summer job for me in the laboratory of the Ft. Worth Water Department, where he worked. The supervisor drew up papers, which would result in my firing if I were still on the job the day after classes started in Austin.

The high school was closed after the graduating class of 1960. My sister Orene is listed as the last graduate of Buckner Academy. The following year the children were bused to public school in Dallas. Since that time the Home, through Buckner Baptist Benevolences, has slowly changed its mission and its character. Most of the land has been sold, and most of the buildings on the main campus have been torn down. The domestic or local mission of the Home is to serve as a foster environment for children while adoptions are finalized. The Alumni Association remains active, but many have become distressed because of the changes and no longer participate in its activities. These alumni feel the changes have left them without an anchor to a way of life that was essential to their development and success in life. It was understood, obviously, that with time those who influenced their development would move on to their final rewards. But the structure and structures that reminded them of their childhoods, to some, as with me, a most satisfying time, are gone. Others feel no reason to support the activities of the Home, but do support the activities of the Association because of its ties to their childhood. As for myself, I have these memories.

Slowly over time I learned the major reasons my mother was so aggressive about my educational opportunities. She had advanced to the ninth grade before leaving school to help support her family, and she told me on more than one occasion our family would have been able to stay together if my father had been better educated. She expressed regret, often, that we had to be raised in the Home. Under the circumstances her decision to place us as she did was the best decision she could have made. I cannot imagine what she went through coming to the conclusions that led to that decision, but without a doubt she agreed with me that it had been made in our best interest. She expressed regret over disruption of traditional family ties, but she did not agonize in our presence over the matter; rather, she continuously stressed education and the importance of family. We all became well educated, and after more than fifty years we remain a close family. I question if the results would have been comparable had she tried to raise us herself. As she was dying at the age of eighty-two, she and I again discussed this issue. She continued to express regret at what had to be done, but finally seemed to be at peace with her decision; or so I have concluded.

To celebrate her seventy-fifth birthday on January 9, 1987, we gathered as a family: her, my siblings and me, children, and grandchildren. There were some sixty-five people who came, in part, to let her know her lessons on education and family had been learned, and to publicly and formally inculcate those lessons into our family conscience as her legacy. We have gathered every year since, moving the date, following her death in 1994, to early December, between her favorite Christian days of worship, Thanksgiving and Christmas, to continue to honor her and her legacy. Her vision of family took a significant jolt when Virginia, known to most as Ginny, and I divorced after eighteen years of marriage. But, with the strong support of the rest of the family, including the children, her vision survives. And the family continues to grow with the introduction in the past year of Mother's first great great-granddaughter, Brooklyn, to accompany her thirteen great-grandchildren and eight grandchildren.

A FRESH LOOK

At the outset this **book** was to be about a unique way of life four of my siblings and I experienced growing up in Buckner Orphans Home. It was to be written **for** our extended family and, perhaps, a few close friends. I designed it to be primarily about my experiences for reasons I have explained in the book. I intended to narrate without being judgmental of the institution in which I was raised.

But along the way I became distracted as I uncovered signs of a developing debate in this country, not yet widely joined, about the value of orphanages in our society (Carr, 2007). Newt Gingrich, Speaker of the House of Representatives in the United States Congress, although probably not starting the debate, certainly contributed significantly to it when he opined in 1995 that orphanages should be reconsidered as an option along with current programs for raising abandoned or discarded or other wise disadvantaged children when foster home systems failed. Segments of the debate have appeared in national news outlets, and testimonials to the value of such institutions are easily found today. Thus, I close these memoirs with my contribution to the dialogue, a summary of the child rearing qualities of the orphanage as I experienced them and to some extent through the eyes of others who lived there.

My conclusions have not been scientifically generated; they come largely from subjective deductions. However, others echo them in a collection of essays written by almost one hundred former inhabitants of Buckner Orphans Home who left in the late 1930s and into the 1970s (Simmons, 2000). They are worthy of respectful attention.

I do not think my siblings and I would have entered our adulthoods with the abilities to cope with the world we found if we had not been raised in Buckner Orphans Home, which we referred to as the Home. Our father had abandoned us. Our mother was too poorly educated to provide for us. Even if we had been placed in foster homes, with relatives or others, the chance we would have stayed together is small. The reasons we were placed in the orphanage are the reasons we would have failed outside it: poverty, ignorance, lack of family stability, lack of education in our mentors, perhaps lack of supervision on the streets.

The most important institutional qualities of which I initially became aware upon entry into the Home were those of security and stability, so important to any unsettled child. I came from a broken home, as did most of the children taken in to the Home. While I did not have to deal with the human pathology of alcoholism, violence, and psychoses from which many of the children were rescued, I do recall the fear of uncertainty. The fact that every day there were guaranteed meals, a place to sleep, and space I could call mine in which I placed my clothes and my personal stuff, was most comforting. Every night I knew where I would be tomorrow and the next day, where I would go to school, and the boundaries of acceptable behavior.

My family was fortunate in that Mother was able to find employment in the orphanage for the first two years of our lives there, easing our acceptance of the place. However, even those who were not similarly blessed, write of the caring nature of most of the adults who were responsible for their well-being, as they settled into the Home (McLeod,

2007). I have chronicled the discipline I received, which was minimal. On the one hand I performed few rebellious acts, which would have jeopardized my place there; on the other there were very few times when I felt mistreated by anyone of authority in the Home, certainly not physically. My life there was during the decade following the Second World War, and most of the supervising adults were of those challenging times. They had experienced adversity and knew how to react to it, with understanding and restraint. I believe all of us benefited by the maturity arising from this honing experience. At Buckner there was nothing remotely resembling the horror stories about orphanages popular in the literature and in the public media during the last century (McKenzie, 1999).

The cadre of supervisors, teachers, and religious leaders, some often one and the same, collectively impressed upon us a common and universal value system, with a defined origin, which we could absorb. The commonality arose from the principles espoused by Baptist teachings of that religious discipline. Some are critical of orphanages for that reason. They complain about evangelicalism and religious indoctrination and the lack of choice of the children in these matters. I think these critics are misguided. Any society, including a relatively closed one as existed during my time at Buckner, needs rules of behavior with commonality to their origin and to their purpose to which children can be exposed as they develop. An institution with 750 children cannot function with varied rules and value systems unique to each person.

The initial question of the critic of the use of religion to define value systems is: should the value systems have their origins in religion? Since the beginning of recorded human history, religion has been the origin of the value systems adopted by man. The admonition, Thou shalt not kill, did not arise from some scientific sociologic survey, or from some philosophical analysis. The next question is: what are the methods with which the procedures and the codes unique to a particular religion are pressed upon the child, the intensity of the application of those methods, and the transparency with which this occurs? Throughout my stay of eight years at Buckner, I was regularly exposed to Christian teachings as rendered by Baptist ministers, and lay people. On Sunday we had church services twice daily. We had worship services on Wednesday evenings during the summer. There were revival services, sometimes daily for two weeks. I do not recall an oppressive atmosphere. In daily life separate from these events, there was no pressure or demand by the authorities we carry these teachings with us, parroting them and their origins on demand, although one was reminded of the value systems in general if one strayed. Thus, hundreds of children could live together without rampant theft, violence, humiliation, and disrespect.

Of course, some deviations from the norm were encountered from time to time; the adults, if the breaches were serious enough, dealt with the perpetrators definitively. But the matter was sometimes also dealt with by the children through, for example, the practice of group rejection, a powerful expression of intolerance that only children can make. Perhaps this latter sanction was the most effective. One of the positive qualities of an institution such as the orphanage is the sense of family, especially to one who had not experienced that closeness before. Once a child discovers that security, there is great reluctance to give it up. Indeed, many of the children, upon leaving the Home, carried with them the value systems extracted from their religious experiences, and patterned their lives accordingly; some crafted their lives' work from these experiences. I see no reason to disqualify the orphanage as a social institution because the admirable results, decent people and good citizens, came from a religious environment.

From my own observations, after the stability the orphanage brought to my life, the next good gift that benefited the children the most was the dedication of the teachers and their inculcation of a work ethic. To a great extent these two qualities go together. Learning is hard work, and dedicated teachers stress that not only academically but also personally. They criticize empathetically and constructively. They demonstrate to each child the importance the progress the child makes as an individual. They expose the child to the rewards of success. I do not recall a single teacher at Buckner who failed to meet these characteristics of a good teacher. And the same can be said of the mentors outside the classroom, at the dairy, the farm, the commissary, and throughout the institution; in some ways all the employees of the Home were teachers. As a result, the achievements of the children after they left the orphanage were generally well above average. Most in my graduating class of twenty-one students in1955 had satisfying careers. Of the ten boys, I know of five who graduated from college, and went on to honorable careers. Two of the top three students in the class achieved doctorial degrees and held important and productive university positions, while the third established himself as an accomplished scientist and administrator in his industry. Similar stories have been reported from other classes graduating from Buckner. I believe this record is directly attributable to the environment of care, discipline, education, and work in which we were raised. It is not over stating the case to declare these achievements especially laudable given the backgrounds of most of the children before they entered Buckner Orphans Home (Simmons, 2000).

I do have one concern regarding the policies of the orphanage to which I was exposed, and that is the policy with which siblings within the institution were dealt. We were segregated according to gender and age. As a result families of siblings were broken up, and often children became closer over time to their peers than to their brothers and sisters. This phenomenon could have a deleterious effect on family life after Buckner. One of my classmates reported to me such an outcome. However, I did not see that in our family. As I have written about this subject at some length, I will not belabor the point. But, it is an issue that should be addressed should the orphanage reemerge as a social institution for raising children. At Buckner when I was there, to allow brothers and sisters to interact across the campus as desired would not have been practical because of the high child to adult ratio and the distances between dormitories. Keeping track of individual children under these circumstances would be a logistical nightmare. Nor would it have been practical to house siblings of the same gender regardless of age. However one approach might have been to structure more time when siblings would have been encouraged to interact as a group in family oriented events such as birthdays, or to sit together in church or at entertainment events. In other words, an official encouragement of family cohesiveness perhaps would have been in order.

In closing, the question should be asked: with the favorable qualities working for it, what happened to the institution? During the last twenty-five or thirty years of the twentieth century a number of orphanages closed or change their missions. For example, Buckner began a mission of outreach internationally and focused on foster care and adoption domestically. Perhaps coincidentally, other institutions also changed at this time. For example, the wholesale discharge of inhabitants from mental institutions into community care became the norm. This process was aided by the success of the pharmaceutical industry in developing medication to dampen the stress of relocation. Unfortunately, there is no pill that can settle the unloved, the unwanted, and the insecure child. Only a family that will bring stability and security into the child's life can accomplish this result. This concept was originally to be the goal of the foster home/adoption programs. Because these programs are not unqualified successes, however, suitable alternatives must be identified (McKenzie, 1999).

Experience in the past with institutions such as Buckner Orphans Home and with programs of today that are strikingly similar to those I and others experienced growing up in Buckner, suggests the concept of the orphanage should seriously be reexamined during the debate over alternate models of childrearing which is underway today. Of course, immediately apparent to anyone who has scrutinized these matters seriously are the changes in our society, legal and social, which would impact on any attempt to create institutions today similar to the orphanages of the past as represented by Buckner Orphans Home of 1950. And those changes are considerable: cost of property, child labor laws, educational requirements in secondary schools, minimal wage laws, teacher union rules, separation of church and state, rights of minors to contract, pervasiveness of advertising and entertainment media, ad infinitum. However, the potential worth of each individual to society makes serious debate worth while.

A TRIBUTE

I have told my stories and have attempted to make the case that the environment in which I was raised in childhood from age nine years old to graduation from high school at the age of seventeen was proper for my needs. But, beyond that I have attempted to establish the proposition that the unique life we experienced in the orphanage known as Buckner Orphans Home was the best for my siblings and me at the time, looking at alternative ways of rearing children. We left the institution with the social and intellectual tools to establish for ourselves and our progeny lives which have been productive and responsible, an outcome that could not have been anticipated before we were taken into Buckner.

I have saluted this result with the following poem presented as a tribute to Buckner Orphans Home, to those within the institution who gave of themselves on behalf of each of us, and to those outside the institution who supported the mission of the Home.

My Home

Without debate or pause
      you took me in.
You gently cradled me
      'til I was calmed.

You bathed
      and clothed me,
and gave me the comforts
      of a bed.

Space to grow,
      you provided me.
You gave me work,
      and fed me.

With care and patience
      you educated me.
And you taught me to
      compete, fairly.

You read to me
      the Golden Rule,
and showed me how
      to use it.

You gave me
      responsibilities,
and new direction
      when I faltered.

In due course
      you honored me,
and then you sent me
      on my way.

Leaving, I knew
      right from wrong,
and that honesty
      eventually prevails.

I knew little of the
      Holocaust or of minorities.
I did know that disrespect
      brings dishonor.

Likewise, I knew little of
      the Silk Road or de Milo.
But I did know it was good
      to ask and learn.

Yes, you saw my needs, by chance,
      and took me in.
And once prepared, you sent me out
      to seek my destiny.

Many times I've been asked,
      what if they took no chance?
The question fades as if unasked,
      because you did.

References

Bullock K. O'D. Homeward Bound. Buckner Baptist Benevolences. 1993.

Carr MR. A Place to Call Home. Prometheus Books. 2007.

McLeod NJW. New and Fortunate Beginnings. 2007.

McKenzie R. Rethinking Orphanages for the 21st Century. Sage Publications. 1999.

Simmons JG (ed). The Orphan Chronicles. Nortex Press. 2000.

About The Author

Clark Watts was born and raised in Dallas, Texas; he is a 1955 high school graduate of Buckner Academy. After receiving a B.A. from The University of Texas at Austin and a Doctor of Medicine degree from the University of Texas Southwestern Medical School, Dallas, he was licensed to practice medicine in Texas in 1962. Following a residency in neurosurgery at Parkland Hospital in Dallas, Texas, he entered private practice in Dallas in 1970 (with neurosurgical Board certification in 1972). Notable among other academic positions, he was Professor of Surgery (Neurosurgery) and Director of the Neurosurgery Residency Program at the University of Missouri in Columbia from 1976 to 1991, with professorship positions at the University of Texas Southwestern Medical School in Dallas (1970-1975), at the University of Maryland School of Medicine in Baltimore (1991-1993), and at the University of Texas Health Science Center in San Antonio (1993-1997). He has held a number of elected and appointed positions in medicine, including President of the Texas Association of Neurological Surgeons (1997-1998) and Editor of *Neurosurgery*, the journal of the Congress of Neurological Surgeons (1982-1987). He received his Juris Doctorate from the University of Missouri in Columbia in 1990, and has been a member of the Texas Bar since 1992. He served twenty-seven years in the U.S. Army Reserves as a general medical officer, neurosurgeon, flight surgeon, advisor on reserve affairs to the Department of Defense, and hospital commander, receiving the Order of Military Medical Merit and the Defense Meritorious Service Medal. He retired in 1998 at the rank of Brigadier General. He retired from medical practice in October 2005. He currently is Adjunct Professor of Law, University of Texas School of Law, Austin, where he has taught since 1996. He and his wife, Patricia, reside in Austin, Texas, with their two English bulldogs, Candy Cane and Al.

Printed in the United States
146990LV00002B/7/P